Eugene Sayre Topping, Father of Trail.

TOPPING'S TRAIL

TOPPING'S TRAIL

ELSIE G. TURNBULL

MITCHELL PRESS LIMITED • VANCOUVER, CANADA

PRINTED IN CANADA
MITCHELL PRESS LIMITED
VANCOUVER, CANADA

TRIBUTE BY A CONTEMPORARY TRAIL EDITOR

COLONEL TOPPING is an enthusiast in whatever he undertakes, business, religion or politics. He is erecting a seventy-five foot pole in front of his real estate office where a flag as large as a pair of blankets tells the people this is Topping's Town and the place where he does his business . . . The Colonel is all right and he don't need fixing either.

CONTENTS

TOPPING'S TRAIL

1.

THE COLONEL TAKES A CHANCE

ALL HIS LIFE the Colonel sought wealth and its accompanying prestige but little dreamed in what manner fate would gratify his ambitions. It was ironic that after years of searching for gold his lucky strike would come as a gift and the summit of his career would be reached when he founded a little smelting town in the wilds of British Columbia. Development of the industry which made the town successful was the work of other men but to Colonel Topping posterity has accorded the title, "Father of Trail". For a time he enjoyed affluence and an honored position before returning to the obscurity and poverty from which he had risen.

He was born Eugene Sayre Topping in 1844, in Suffolk County of New York State. Little is known of his early life except that at the age of eleven he joined the crew of a sailing vessel and visited many ports of the world. Ten years later his desire for adventure led him to the western plains of the United States at the time of railway construction across the continent. In 1867 the Union Pacific was laying track in Wyoming and Topping joined the work crew. Two years later, when the line was completed, he decided to remain in Wyoming and prospect for gold in the Yellowstone River area.[1]

[1] Trail Creek News, January 26, 1917.

Then a youth of twenty-five, he was tall and rangy with jet black hair and sharp eyes. His wiry frame was well adapted for the rough life of the wilderness and for a while he led a life of trapping, prospecting and fighting Indians.

In the summer of 1872, Topping accompanied an expedition from the United States Geological Survey which was exploring the headwaters of the Yellowstone River. A few days after the group left the Mammoth Hot Springs, Topping and a companion ascended the Gardiner River on a search for new wonders. Climbing a mountain, they spent the night on the heights and at daylight saw an immense column of steam rising into the air far to the south. They set out to find it and finally reached a great geyser area now known as the Norris Basin, lying on the Gibbon Fork of the Firehole River.

On another summer expedition Topping and a friend packed in whipsaw, canvas and rigging to Yellowstone Lake and built a sloop for use in collecting specimens from the Park. Prospecting journeys were not successful, so Topping turned to wolfing in order to make a livelihood. Strychnine-filled buffalo carcasses were laid as bait for the wolves which were then left to freeze, the trappers returning to skin them during the first spring thaw. Thousands of pelts could be secured in a season, but the trade was hampered by hostile Indians who resented white men entering their country.

In the winter of 1874 Topping and his companions were besieged in their log cabin on the Little Big Horn by a band of Uncapapas and only escaped by slipping downriver after dark. Refuge was found in the military establishment of Fort Pease which was situated on the Yellowstone River at the mouth of the Big Horn. Skirmishing between Sioux and whites continued, resulting in General Custer's Massacre and the retaliatory expedition of General Crook, when the Indians were finally defeated. Topping reportedly acted as scout for General Crook in some of his campaigns and it is probable that these experiences led to his receiving the title of "Colonel". This easy acquisition of rank was common at the time in the west.

3

At this time Topping began writing a series of articles on the Indian wars for eastern newspapers. Collecting stories of traders, explorers, surveyors in Wyoming, he amassed details for Hubert Howe Bancroft, the California bookseller who was engaged in writing his monumental history of the western United States. Topping himself made use of this material in a book he published under the title, "Chronicles of the Yellowstone".[2] Written in an easy, comprehensive style, it shows literary ability, a gift which one of Topping's sisters also possessed for she is said to have been a "graceful writer."[3]

Not yet successful in finding his gold mine, Topping pushed farther west. He crossed the Rocky Mountains to the Coeur d'Alene district of northern Idaho where the fabulous Bunker Hill and Sullivan had recently been uncovered. Luck still eluded him but tales of rich strikes along the shores of Kootenay Lake in British Columbia enticed him to a new camp in a new country.

In 1886 the Silver King mine showing had been discovered high on Toad Mountain and a small camp sprang up on the edge of Kootenay Lake. In turn called both Salisbury and Stanley, it finally was named Nelson. When Topping made his way to this spot two years later he found six log cabins and a cluster of tents between Cottonwood and Ward Creeks. Twice weekly a twin-screw steamer brought supplies and mail from Bonner's Ferry and returned laden with sacks of ore from the Silver King.[4]

Topping liked the camp. He quickly made friends with an American family newly arrived from Illinois — Frank Hanna, his wife Mary Jane and their four children. Christmas dinner of 1888 he enjoyed in the cozy Hanna cabin.

Then one day, while stooping to get a drink from a creek, Topping accidentally discharged his gun, wounding his wrist severely. Unable to continue prospecting he obtained the position of deputy mining recorder after taking out papers as a

[2] Chronicles of the Yellowstone by E. S. Topping.
[3] Trail Creek News, March 12, 1897.
[4] British Columbia, Vol. II by F. W. Howay and E. O. S. Scholefield.

Canadian citizen. He was now a paid official in a prosperous camp and his future seemed assured.[5]

Colonel Topping was content with his lot but fortune had other plans for him. As he sat in his office on a hot July day in 1890, two prospectors entered to record claims they had staked on Red Mountain, fifty miles away. Joe Moris and Joe Bourgeois had been working the Lily May, a prospect on Deer Park Mountain where the Dewdney Trail crossed the Rossland Range to drop down to the Columbia River, when they noticed a red outcrop on the hill across the valley.

Upon investigation they put stakes on four claims and an extension, naming them War Eagle, Centre Star, Virginia, Idaho and LeWise. Since the law forbade staking more than one claim on the same vein they offered Topping the extension if he would pay recording dues for all five claims. Ever a gambler, Topping agreed to pay the fee of twelve dollars and fifty cents in return for ownership of the LeWise location. Its name he changed to LeRoi. At last he had found his mine.[6]

The more Topping examined his claim the more optimistic he became. All indications pointed to a large ore body and assays were excellent. Red Mountain was six miles above the Columbia River and the only way ore could be brought out was by pack train down the valley of Trail Creek. Then it would have to be loaded on the sternwheeler *Lytton* recently put on the Columbia to run from Northport to Sproat's Landing. Topping saw an opportunity for business at the steamboat landing; so he and his friend, Frank Hanna, pre-empted three hundred and forty-three acres of land at the mouth of Trail creek. Pitching a tent among the trees the Colonel prepared to stay while Hanna returned to Nelson to move his family. Twenty packhorses carried the party and their possessions over the narrow trail from Nelson to Sproat's Landing where transfer was made to the *Lytton*. What Mary Jane Hanna

[5] Trail Creek News, Oct. 2, 1896, Oct. 23, 1896.
[6] First History of Rossland by Harold Kingsmill and B.C. Mines Report for 1896.

thought when she first caught sight of the little tent standing alone in the empty stretch of forest can only be imagined, but they all disembarked and scrambled up the stony beach to begin life in this lonely spot.[7]

Hanna quickly set to work to provide a more adequate home than the tent and by the time winter came they were comfortably settled in a two-storeyed log cabin which they dubbed "Trail House". To the children there was fascination in forest and river. It was always exciting to see the *Lytton* churning against the current, ready to catch the eddy at the right moment and swing into the landing. She brought supplies for sale to prospectors — food, picks and shovels, and cases of whiskey to be dispensed at the bar. Many passengers disembarking spent the night at the Trail House before going up the hill to the mines. It was Jane Hanna's responsibility to feed and lodge these travellers. Wood for the stoves and fireplace came from the forest, water from the creek. Facilities were primitive but Jane managed to achieve comfort for her family and guests. Across from the house, Frank built a rough blacksmith shop where he could shoe horses and sharpen tools as required.

The winter of 1890-91 passed quickly and suddenly it was spring. On the evening of March fifth, great excitement prevailed in Trail House. Jane gave birth to twin girls whom she named Molly and Lydia. It was an event calling for celebration, for they were the first white babies born at the Landing and the first white twins in the whole West Kootenay. Everyone rejoiced and away off in Victoria, John Houston of Nelson wrote of the occurrence: "Born at Trail, to Mr. and Mrs. F. Hanna, twins—girls. Mother and children doing well. The Father has done well." [8] Jane was now really busy but she managed to secure a helper, a Miss Hill, who came to live with them and to act as governess for the older children.[9]

[7] Trail Creek News, April 25, 1896.
[8] Trail Creek News, March 7, 1903.
[9] Susie McClung Inghram—Memoirs written in 1936.

Meanwhile Colonel Topping had been occupied with his mining property. When word of the first find spread abroad prospectors flocked to the hills around Red Mountain. All during the summer of 1890 claims were staked — Iron Horse, Number One, Gertrude, Columbia, Monte Cristo, Iron Colt, Gopher, Crown Point, Nickel Plate, Kootenay, Cliff, Evening Star, Jumbo and Consolidated St. Elmo.[10]

In the autumn Colonel Topping left for Spokane, laden with samples from the LeRoi. Travelling on the railroad from Northport he met two Spokane lawyers, George Forster and Colonel W. N. Ridpath, who were much impressed with his samples and introduced him to interested associates in Spokane. Topping was able to persuade this group to take a bond on sixteen-thirtieths of his property for the sum of sixteen thousand dollars. Oliver Durant, a mining man of considerable experience, inspected the claim and sank a shaft. In the spring of '91 he packed ten tons of ore over the snow to the Columbia River and shipped them to the Colorado Smelting Works in Butte. Returns were excellent; so the group took up the bond and organized the LeRoi Gold Mining Company, registering it in Spokane, Washington. Forster was named president of the company, W. Williams, secretary, and directors included George Turner, Col. W. W. Turner, Col. Ridpath, Col. I. N. Peyton, Oliver Durant, Alexander Tarbet, W. J. Harris and Major Armstrong. They also bought Topping's remaining share in the mine. Thus the Colonel sold for thirty thousand dollars a mine which would later command a price of three million and for which he had paid twelve dollars and fifty cents. It was typical of his ebullient nature that he never admitted regret for his action but always said he would find another just as good.

For more than a year Durant developed the LeRoi, but then sold his interest and with Tarbet bonded the Centre Star and War Eagle. Through his efforts a trail from Northport was opened and the provincial government built a wagon road

[10] Drysdale—Geology and Ore Deposits of Rossland.

from the mines to Trail Creek Landing. Although narrow and rutted, its surface pocked with boulders and the occasional stump, the road enabled four-horse teams to haul ore down to the Columbia. There, Topping and Hanna built a small shack for storage of the ore while awaiting shipment.

Eighteen ninety-three was a year of depression in the United States. Business slumped and several Spokane banks suspended payment. Durant and Tarbet were forced to give up their bond on the War Eagle properties while the LeRoi closed temporarily.[11]

To add to the gloom, disaster struck at Trail Creek Landing. The spring of '94 was one of great flooding by the Columbia River. With an appalling ferocity it swept over the flats, pushing up Trail Creek to the foot of Lookout Mountain. Topping and the Hannas watched helplessly as the angry waters carried away their home and most of their possessions. Only the ore depot stood firm, held down by the weight of rock stored within. This was a serious blow but when the river subsided construction of a new building was begun, this time on higher ground. Ready for opening by Christmas of '94, the new Trail House was frankly a hotel. It was ninety feet long, two storeys in height and contained a dining room, a saloon, a post-office and sleeping room for fifty guests.[12]

Meanwhile prospects in Rossland Camp brightened. Large ore bodies were uncovered in the LeRoi and the first dividends were paid in 1895. During the preceding summer the War Eagle properties were bonded to Wakefield, Roberts and Corbin of Spokane who took Patrick Clark and J. A. Finch into the partnership. After a careful survey of the workings, it was found that the tunnel had not followed the ore vein. A crosscut was made to reach the vein which showed such richness it proved the War Eagle was undoubtedly a mine. In December Clark and his associates paid off the bond at a price of twenty-three thousand dollars and made a contract with the East Helena

---

[11] B.C. Mines Report, 1896.
[12] Trail Creek News, Oct. 19, 1895.

Montana Smelting Company to supply one thousand tons of ore each month. This deal received much publicity in news-papers and attention focussed again on Rossland Camp. "In January 1895 nearly every well-known prospector in the north-west was heading for Trail Creek and by the middle of March every available piece of ground had been located." [13] The *Lytton,* making her daily run from Northport, was crowded with passengers and in the summer she was joined by the *Nakusp* which made connection with the main line of the Canadian Pacific at Arrowhead.

Among the hundreds who came to the area in the summer of '95 were three men — James Breen, a mining engineer, J. D. Farrell, a railroad man, and a promoter named A. E. Humphries. They inspected the Rossland mines, checked the feasibility of a tramway up Trail Creek valley and inspected the townsite owned by Topping and Hanna. Topping soon discovered they represented a mining magnate who was considering installation of a smelter in the district. The Colonel enthusiastically offered them a site of forty acres on a bench above the Columbia River for the smelter and a two-thirds interest in the townsite of Trail. When Breen obtained a con-tract from the LeRoi Mining Company for 37,500 tons of ore and the promise of a further 37,500 tons, the deal was concluded. Humphries and Breen then revealed they were agents for F. Augustus Heinze of Butte, Montana.

Augustus Heinze had been born in Brooklyn in 1869, of German-Irish parentage. After graduating from the Columbia School of Mines, he had worked in Butte. A timely legacy en-abled him to organize the Montana Ore Purchasing Company and to build a smelter in Butte. By devious means he acquired extensive properties and in 1895 was just beginning his spec-tacular career of litigation against the copper tycoons of Butte, Marcus Daly and Wm. A. Clark.

Ever on the lookout for ore, Heinze had sent his emissaries to investigate the Rossland mines. When they reported

---

[13] First History of Rossland by Harold Kingsmill.

possibilities he moved with characteristic decision into the field of Canadian mining. Late in the summer of '95 he began construction of a copper smelter in Topping's townsite.[14]

In after years the Colonel was fond of saying he had envisioned a smelter in his first glimpse of Trail flats. "I saw," he said, "that ores from the mines where Rossland has since grown must be smelted in this country. The ores must come down hill to the river and there, all ready-made above the Columbia, was a perfect site for a smelter.[15]

[14] War of the Copper Kings by Glasscock.
[15] Trail Creek News.

2.

A TOWN IS BORN

O N A SUNNY day in early Oc-
tober, 1895, Colonel Topping stepped from his office in Trail
House to get a breath of air. All day the tiny room where he and
Hanna carried on their real estate business had been crowded
with men anxious to buy lots in the new town. People had
swarmed to the Landing as soon as smelter construction started,
buying any possible lot whether it was stump-strewn or still
covered with pine trees. To them it did not matter. They would
soon clear enough ground to erect a log shack or tent where they
could secure some of the business bound to come to a smelter
town. As the Colonel stood at the door in the fresh warm air he
could hear the constant sound of hammers and shovels and
could glimpse a rude building or two in process of construction.
His town was at last coming into existence and the future
looked very bright.

Directly across the Trail Creek draw he could see the boxlike Crown Point Hotel. It was not yet finished but already
people were staying there, sleeping on the floors of its bare
rooms. In July, S. F. Petersen had bought three lots at the
corner of Bayview and Spokane streets and built a shack where
he and his carpenters could live as they worked. By August
they were laying the floor of the hotel, called the Crown Point
after the big mine on Lake Mountain. In September, Petersen's

brother John arrived with his wife Laura and daughter Anna, whose first glimpse of Trail revealed newcomers camping on the stony banks of the Columbia. Later a third brother, Julius, joined the hotel management.

As the Colonel looked around, his eye met the old shack built for storage of ore from the LeRoi mine. Now it was neatly fixed up to accommodate Steele and McDonald's general store. At the foot of Smelter Hill, Peter Genelle had built a portable sawmill while downriver the Colonel could see the lot he had just sold to Bell and Naden for another sawmill. Much lumber was needed for all the construction work and the sternwheelers could not import enough. Across from Trail House the Colonel could hear the rattle of dishes inside the tent which served as James Clinton's I.X.L. restaurant, and Jimmie's singsong greeting as he offered the best twenty-five cent meal in Trail: "Good afternoon, gentlemen! We have the ham, the egg, the loin, the sirloin, the round, the chop, the mutton steak, the mocha and the java to come along and the famous Irish stew to follow!"

In the draw below the Crown Point, W. H. Johnson ("Good Old Brown") was busily moulding bricks. Behind the hotel, Raymond and Comstock provided stables for forty horses while Billy Noonan worked from dawn to dusk shoeing the dozens of horses needed for hauling of supplies. Under the brow of the hill near the riverbank Charlie Ross had installed two tubs in a shack where baths might be taken any hour of the day or night. Charlie also delivered water in a barrel wagon all over town. Nearby, Lee Chung had completed a log house for use as a laundry.

Nor had the Townsite Company been idle. It had laid out rough streets and roadways and had begun work on the Bowery Bridge spanning the mouth of Trail Creek. The Colonel was impatient to finish the bridge for the gulley was wide and deep and cut the settlement into two distinct areas. From where he stood he could see that Hanna and his crew of men were making progress.

Plans for the future kept racing through Topping's mind.

Trail House was full to overflowing with guests and the office where he and Hanna conducted their business was much too small. They must build a more imposing place and the Colonel could see the right location for it down Bayview Avenue. There they would erect a structure big enough to contain a post-office, telephone office and a few stores, with a second storey which could be used as an Opera House. Something must be done for Jane Hanna, too. She had a new baby, Estella, and she had been worried the last few days about Frankie, Jr. The boy had a bilious fever and was far from well. She deserved a house for her family and the Colonel considered an ideal site to be a bench overlooking the business section of the growing town.

The shrill whistle of the steamer *Lytton* cut short the Colonel's reverie. He watched as Captain Nesbitt swung the churning vessel alongside the beach and threw out a gangplank for passengers to disembark. The Colonel strolled down to welcome them to his town. A jaunty man warmly shook his outstretched hand and greeted him with enthusiasm.

"W. F. Thompson is my name, sir. From Sprague, Washington, lately of the Sprague Independent, I've come to start the only home-print newspaper in the Kootenay country!"

Thompson proved full of energy. In a short time he rounded up some helpers and hewed out a rough home for his newspaper, the Trail Creek News, whose avowed purpose was a "weekly published in the interests of the Trail Creek mining region and for the financial advancement of its proprietor." Using a shovel, an axe and a hatchet, the men raised a shack, primitive but adequate. A latch string secured the door which opened beautifully but required two men to close. To open a window, a board was removed from the side wall and to replenish the stove Thompson reached out and tore down a small sapling. He had brought a Washington handpress with him but paper was delayed. Nothing daunted, Thompson borrowed wrapping paper from the grocery store and issued the first copy of the Trail Creek News on October 19. Apology was made: "The News has no desire to appear remarkable save in its capacity as a news conveyor and did not expect to greet you in its initial number with clothes on that would look better encircling a yard of calico." [1]

Meanwhile the smelter was gradually taking shape. Stonemasons were busy on foundations while carpenters and bricklayers worked long hours. From the steamer landing at the foot of the hill cordwood was hoisted up an inclined tramway to be stockpiled in the yard. Supplies were also ferried across the Columbia at the terminus of a road built to connect with the Nelson & Fort Sheppard railway at Sayward. Contractors for the building job were Anderson and Costello, while the superintendent of the whole project was James Breen, the mining engineer from Butte. Young Mr. Breen was a popular addition to the devotees of the Trail House bar, when he joined them of an evening. Things were progressing wonderfully, he reported. Ore platforms were almost ready for shipments from the LeRoi. The plant would consist of a sampling works capable of handling ten tons per hour and a smelting department with one water-jacket furnace and two matteing furnaces which could process one hundred and fifty tons a day, also a calcining plant for both ores and matte. A brick stack, one hundred and thirty-five feet in height, would carry off the fumes.

In the midst of all the activity and bustling growth of the new settlement death struck suddenly. One evening in mid-October, as the *Lytton* pulled away from the landing, a man splashed into the river. Rodney Robinson, startled by the boat's searchlight, had stepped backward into the Columbia. Chief Engineer Hector Sproat leaped after him, but was hampered by a padded jacket and heavy shoes. Struggling with Robinson, he was unable to grasp ropes thrown to him by bystanders. Then Peter Genelle ran into the water and thrust a board to Sproat who grabbed it and the two men were hauled ashore. The unconscious Robinson was carried into Trail House but despite all efforts died a few hours later. Colonel Topping now had reason to include a cemetery in

[1] Trail Creek News, October 19, 1895.

his townsite. Far beyond the town's boundaries, he obtained two acres on the bench beyond the smelter. Robinson was friendless and destitute, so Topping arranged for his funeral and conducted a simple burial service while several ladies sang "Rock of Ages."

A month later the Colonel took part in a second funeral, this one closer to his heart. Sixteen-year old Frankie Hanna, who had lain ill of typhoid for two weeks, succumbed to the disease. A long procession of mourners in carriages, on horse-back and afoot, followed the white velvet casket to its resting place in the new cemetery on Smelter Flats.

Death had visited the community twice within a month but in early December the first male birth took place when a son was born to Mr. and Mrs. W. O. Sanford. Christened LeRoi, he became known as Trail's mascot.

Thanksgiving came and passed without celebration, for no minister had as yet arrived in the little settlement. However, Christmas was not to go unnoticed and plans were laid for a monster party and Trail's first Ball. On December 24th the newly built Topping Hanna Block was gay with green boughs and a huge tree laden with gifts. Squeals of delight were heard as the children gathered in the dusk of late after-noon. Santa Claus appeared and took from the tree a present for each child. Much merriment broke forth when he called the name "Eugene Sayre Topping" and the Colonel stepped up to receive a large doll and a merry-go-round.

Christmas Day was given to feasting in hotels and private homes. On Christmas night the Grand Ball was held but only thirty couples appeared to dance to the music of Sumpf's orchestra and to eat the elaborate wine supper served at mid-night. When a Rossland newspaper hinted that the affair had been a failure the Editor of the News replied defiantly, "Next year our citizens will give another Ball. Trail will be a city of ten thousand by that time and the attendance will be larger than on the occasion in question." [3]

2 Trail Creek News, Nov. 22, 1895.
3 Trail Creek News, Dec. 27, 1895.

After Christmas the Hanna family and Colonel Topping moved into the big cottage built by the Townsite Company for Mrs. Hanna. She was its owner and received board money from both her husband Frank and the Colonel. The new house was beautiful. Standing on the first bench of Lookout Mountain at the corner of Farwell and Tamarac avenues, it boasted spacious rooms with wide windows, and even a bathroom! Water was piped from a spring in the hills. The Colonel had suggested that window sash be painted vermilion but Jane refused emphatically. She preferred black casings against the buff-colored frame house with its white cornices. However she made no objection to a flagpole in the yard bearing a big Canadian flag. Come spring, she planned an extensive garden of fruit trees and strawberry plants, bordered with flowers.

From the corner room which he occupied the Colonel could overlook the whole area of his town. He could see the Hanna Block, housing post-office and telephone office, the Madden House, the St. Elmo which proudly claimed to be the "only plastered hotel in Trail" and the Wellington, run by Andy Hughes who inspired a pious wish on the part of the News editor: "May the genial Andy always have it full and never be full himself." At the foot of Spokane street Editor Thompson had built a log cabin with a cupola on its roof and a bear den in its yard, inhabited by a brown bear cub, "the size of five pounds of lard and as full of wood ticks as Trail is full of embryo millionaires."

When the Colonel's gaze wandered to the left it encountered the long frame structure of the smelter with its square brick stack cutting the skyline. The Colonel liked the owner of the smelter, young twenty-six year old Fritz Heinze. Affable, debonair, a good mixer, Heinze knew what he wanted and always moved swiftly to attain it. True, he brooked no opposition and the Colonel had been disturbed when in mid-December Heinze had ordered Jim Breen back to Butte. Breen was responsible for design of the plant and had erected it in record time despite difficulties. Everyone was sorry to see him leave but Heinze came to Trail bringing H. C. Bellinger as new manager and Topping saw that there would be no looking back. Fritz was a go-getter, a man of action, "without a small idea in his head." With such a man the smelter was bound to be successful and Topping resolved that the town would progress as well.

On the first of February in 1896 the furnace was blown in, with Colonel Topping accompanying the group of officials who drove up the snowy hill to attend the opening ceremony. They inspected the bins filled with LeRoi ore, ready for roasting on great piles of cordwood in the smelter yard. Several days previously these heaps had been fired and thick yellow smoke now hung over the town. To-day for the first time horsedrawn cars transferred the roasted ores to the blast furnace where they would burn before emerging as copper matte. Trail was at last a smelter town.[4]

[4] Trail Creek News, February 8, 1896.

3.

TRAIL IS THE TOWN WHERE SMELTERS GROW

With the blowing in of the British Columbia Smelting and Refining Company's first furnace, prosperity came to Trail Creek and for the next one and one-half years progress was phenomenal. Editor Thompson expressed it thus when celebrating his newspaper's six months' existence: "In some sections newspapers have but one birthday anniversary each year, but six months' life in Trail is equal to a year in any other town." [1]

Ore for the smelter was hauled from the LeRoi mine in big horse-drawn freight wagons but Heinze soon turned his attention to the construction of a narrow-gauge tramway from the boat landing to the Rossland mines. Shortly after Christmas of 1895 F. P. Gutelius arrived in Trail to superintend the work. Grading went ahead rapidly and while snow still lay on the ground, rails were laid along the waterfront and a frame depot built. In April the steamer *Arrowhead* brought a scowload of rolling stock, consisting of an engine and four ore cars purchased from the Dunmore and Lethbridge line in Alberta. Fires were lighted in the locomotive and after a few trial runs over the greasy track the work of forwarding ties and rails was begun. One quarter to one half mile was

[1] Trail Creek News, March 28, 1896.

laid daily and by June the line was ready for use between Trail and Rossland. Service started with two daytime trains each way and a night train. More rolling stock was purchased from the Utah Northern Railway—eleven flatcars, six boxcars, an engine and a private coach which had belonged to John W. Young (a son of Brigham Young) when he was president of the Mormon line. Remodelled, one-half being used as a drawing room, it was used by Heinze on his frequent visits to Trail.[2]

Colonel Topping, meanwhile, was immersed in town affairs. His spare, jaunty figure was seen everywhere as he strolled, cane in hand, flower in his buttonhole and cigar in his mouth. Now a man of fifty-two, he looked much younger, perhaps because his thick hair and drooping moustache were still very black. Photographs show a touch of melancholy, quite belying his buoyant nature and optimistic faith in the value of his mines and real estate. It was reported that he was offered seventy-five thousand dollars for a mine which he refused because he considered it a second LeRoi and intended to hold it until he could get a million dollars or more for it.[3]

After quitting Trail House he severed his business connection with Frank Hanna and set up an office on the Bowery. A Canadian flag graced the front of the one-storey building where he sold real estate and offered to "examine and report on mines, bringing to bear on the latter the result of twenty-eight years of experience in mining." He offered for sale claims on Beaver Creek and the Salmon River, in the Lardeau and on Murphy Creek. Many of his prospects were on Lookout Mountain, that gently rounded peak rising above the town of Trail, while up the Arrow Lake at Deer Park he joined Petersen brothers in acquiring land for a townsite and in developing the Bluebird and the Boston Boy. They built a hotel and planned a sawmill and a tug for the lake. Business flourished and the Colonel's nephew, James Worth, came from New York to serve as clerk in his uncle's office.[4]

[2] Trail Creek News, April 4, 1896, June 12, 1896, Oct. 23, 1896.
[3] Trail Creek News, May 2, 1896.
[4] Trail Creek News, April 16, 1897, Nov. 27, 1896, May 9, 1896.

When Heinze came to Trail he had been given a one-third interest in the Townsite Company while Humphries and associates had purchased another third. The company now decided to dissolve and early in April the shareholders met to divide the property. Lot numbers were placed in a box. Each man withdrew a slip while Jimmie Anderson entered the new owner's name and number in a book. It proved a slow job and when forty lots were still to be apportioned Heinze suggested a game of draw poker for the entire remainder. Topping and the others agreed with alacrity and the game was on. Fortune swayed back and forth with ownership of valuable Trail property depending on the turn of a card. Both Topping and Heinze were always gamblers but Heinze seemed to ride on the crest of good luck. In a final hand he won the pot and emerged the winner of sixteen thousand dollars of realty. Heinze turned his property over to Lee Davenport to sell, Humphries to the R. J. Bealy Company while Topping handled his own, announcing in the newspaper: "The Townsite Company is no more. Exit one, entrez trois. Yet the sale of lots goes on. I have choice ones and cheap ones for sale." [5]

After his break with Hanna, Topping associated himself with a newcomer from Spokane, Richard Tevia Daniel. A true soldier of fortune, Daniel had been born in Kentucky but had come to the West at an early age and amassed considerable wealth. In later years he was fond of telling how, without a dollar, he arrived in Spokane when it was a village of three hundred inhabitants. After working on the Northern Pacific Railway, he saved enough to buy a livery stable which enabled him to provide packhorses for the Coeur d'Alene mining boom. With his profits he bought real estate in downtown Spokane, an investment that would yield rich returns. Attracted by the promise of the Trail district, he purchased mines on Lookout Mountain and city property known as Columbia Heights. Illiterate, boastful, he was full of confidence and willing to tackle anything that promised financial returns.

[5] Trail Creek News, April 4, 1896, April 11, 1896.

The first project undertaken by Topping and Daniel was that of supplying water to the new town. Up Gorge Creek they built several dams and a reservoir, considering the elevation sufficient to force water anywhere it was needed. Four hydrants were provided in the downtown area for dousing fires.

Topping and Daniel then turned their attention to the erection of a big bridge over Trail Creek. Meandering across the flat to enter the Columbia behind the Crown Point Hotel, the creek divided the settlement and in times of flood spread in a lake over the low-lying land at the base of Smelter Hill. The Townsite Company had spanned it with the Bowery bridge close to its mouth but business men now wanted a longer structure reaching from Victoria Avenue to Spokane street, at a height of twenty feet above low water. No government money was available so Topping and Daniel canvassed citizens for funds. Response was generous and during high water of '96 logs were floated up the creek and piledrivers set to work. Several further appeals for money were needed before the big wooden bridge was finished in the spring of '97. When completed, it united the two parts of the town and provided a wide space for promenading, for parades and for horse racing. It was a source of pride to the townspeople. Every plank, rail and spike was paid for out of the pockets of the local citizens.[6]

Daniel also entered the hotel business by building the four-storey Arlington at the corner of Spokane and Bay streets. Surmounted by a conical tower at one corner and furnished with the best fittings obtainable, it was hailed by Lieutenant-Governor Dewdney as the "finest hotel in the West".[7]

Hotel construction went on apace during the year. Blake and Hector opened the Victoria while Fred Kaiser built the Kaiser Hotel across from the Trail House. In July, Mrs. Mary Ann Meakin erected the three-storey Meakin Hotel at the corner of Spokane and Cedar Avenue. A plump fifty-year-old woman who resembled Queen Victoria, she ran an establishment "filled with cool breezes and choice viands." In her past she had

[6] Trail Creek News, May 16, 1896.
[7] Trail Creek News, Sept. 11, 1896.

been an expert needlewoman and in her up-stairs parlor she hung two pictures done in brilliant needlepoint for which she had won prizes in the Montreal Exposition of 1881.[8]

All these hotels provided an opportunity for local brewing of beer. Early in the year, Fritz Sick of Spokane built a brewery in Dublin Gulch, installing a copper kettle with a capacity of fifteen barrels and by spring the first home-brewed Imperial Lager was served at saloon bars. At first, delivery was made in a basket on the arm, then in a handcart but soon a wagon drawn by a sleek gray horse made morning calls at the hotels.[9]

Meanwhile essential services were appearing in the town. Deputy-postmaster Frank Brown kept agitating for a school and after the New Year forty children were assembled in the Hanna Block for classes. Frank Hanna, having a large family, was interested in education. He marshalled volunteer labor to build a small schoolhouse on the bench above his home. Roughly constructed, it was full of knot holes through which the pupils could gaze at the outside world while cracks in the flooring tempted them to drop pencils on the ground below. A forest fire in the summer destroyed the building but it was replaced by a two-room schoolhouse whose cost was paid with a grant from the Provincial Government. By autumn one hundred children were in attendance, taught by Principal Donald Dewar and Mabel Grace Bunting.[10]

In January of 1896 the first doctor arrived in Trail — young unmarried Dr. W. T. Hoyes. He was followed by Dr. Douglas Corsan who was appointed physician for the smelter and tramway companies. Dr. Corsan built a combined residence and hospital at the corner of Cedar and Helena streets, containing living quarters for the doctor's family and a ward with eight hospital beds, an operating room, a balcony for convalescents and a large bathroom. It cost four thousand dollars and was quite the most elaborate dwelling in Trail.[11]

[8] Trail Creek News, July 3, 1896.
[9] Trail Creek News, Nov. 29, 1895, Mar. 14, Aug. 7, 1896.
[10] Trail Creek News, Nov. 29, 1895, Jan. 4, Mar. 28, 1896.
[11] Trail Creek News, Jan. 25, May 16, Dec. 11, 1896.

Spiritual needs were not neglected. Reverend Henry Irwin, the famous Father Pat, had just been put in charge of mission work in Rossland for the Church of England. Soon after arrival he arranged to hold services in the Hanna Block. However he failed to appear while a large congregation waited patiently. It seems that on the snowy road downhill from Rossland he had stopped to play the kind Samaritan to a teamster in distress. This was quite consistent with the character of Father Pat who was ever mindful of the unfortunate, the ill and the underprivileged. On first coming to British Columbia from his native Ireland he had served in construction camps of the Canadian Pacific Railway and endeared himself to all for his kindness and interest in human suffering. Now he would minister to the miners in Rossland and also conduct a weekly service in the settlement of Trail.

Spring saw the arrival of the Reverend A. McMillan, a minister of the Presbyterian faith. He began construction of a small church on Spokane street which when finished in the late summer was used by all denominations. But one board in thickness, it was cold and draughty in winter weather and worshippers sat huddled in coats and overshoes.

Churches for the other religious groups were not built until later. At the corner of Pine and Farwell the Methodists built a church which was ready for Easter services of 1897 conducted by Rev James Ferris. In June Emmanuel Baptist Church opened its doors on Eldorado near Pine with the Reverend T. A. P. Fost as minister while a Roman Catholic Congregation erected a meeting place near the brewery.[12] Father Revers of Rossland took it under his charge. Although an Anglican mission had been organized by Father Pat, St. Andrew's Church was not consecrated until November, 1898. Its first rector, Reverend William Clark, arrived during the summer and found accomodation in a tent.

In a town of wooden buildings, fire protection was imperative. As early as the autumn of '95 a volunteer fire brigade

[12] Trail Creek News, Feb. 8, 1896, Aug. 14, 1896, April 16, 1897, June 11, 1897, Aug. 6, 1897.

was organized with J. E. McCarthy as Chief. Several balls were held to raise money for equipment. Nozzles, hose and a cart were purchased, also a bell which was mounted on the roof of the Trail Stables. Instructions advised anyone discovering a fire to discharge his pistol in four rapid reports while whoever was near the bell should pull the rope for fifteen minutes until the volunteers appeared with the cart.[13] It was not until 1898 that the small square firehall with its 50-foot tower was built where the railroad tracks crossed Bay Avenue Bridge.

Some measure of police protection was afforded in the summer of '96 when B. Abernathy was hired as constable. In September he was succeeded by William J. Devitt, an ex-North West Mounted policeman from Calgary. Topping thought the provincial government should provide a courthouse and jail and he wrote a series of letters about the subject. His efforts resulted in the erection of a lockup on the lane behind Cedar Avenue near Helena street. It was a neat cottage containing four cells, equipped with bars, bolts and big locks. Chief Devitt soon had his prisoners busy planting grass and building a fence around the yard where the Canadian flag waved aloft.[14]

It was not until the spring of '97 that the Bank of British North America established a branch office in Trail with David Doig as manager. Until that time the R. J. Bealy Co. handled all banking business. Their first local manager was Jimmie Anderson who was "banker, insurance agent, express agent, notary public, conveyancer, real estate agent, agent for Columbia & Kootenay Steam Navigation Company and Canadian Pacific Railway customs broker." George Naden succeeded Anderson in March, 1896, staying for a year when he was followed by H. E. Robertson. Robertson later was drowned in the Columbia when his canoe upset in a riffle. In September of '96 a young man from Nova Scotia came to Bealy's as clerk. He was Thomas Wentworth Bingay and the future would

[13] Trail Creek News, Feb. 15, 1896, Feb. 22, 1896, Feb. 29, 1896.
[14] Trail Creek News, July 3, 1896, Sept. 4, 1896, Dec. 3, 1897.

see him as an influential figure in the smelter when he became chief accountant.[15]

In the spring of '97 electricity replaced coal-oil lamps in Trail. At five minutes past five o'clock on the afternoon of April 6, Fred Hoffmeister turned on the water in a power-house built on Pine Avenue at the base of Smelter Hill. A big Pelton wheel started to revolve; electric lights flashed on in the smelter and two hundred incandescent bulbs gleamed through the dusk. Later in the evening the current was sent along the wire to business places in Trail, while a crowd gathered at the Crown Point Hotel to admire the working of the new system.

F. Augustus Heinze had built the new powerhouse. Water came by flume from Trail and Stoney creeks to drop down Smelter Hill at a head of three hundred and fifty feet and discharge into Trail Creek near the corner of Pine and Victoria. Within the powerhouse two Pelton wheels, thirty-six inches in diameter generated four hundred horsepower which provided light for both smelter and town.[16]

During all this time of progress Colonel Topping was a very busy man, yet he found leisure to organize a baseball club and a brass band. Turning out to practise with the ball players, he proved the best man on the team. They elected him an honorary member and he contributed generously to the purchase of uniforms, blue in color with caps, belts and stockings of maroon.[17] For the band he headed a subscription list to buy instruments and secured a leader. It was a happy addition to parades and excursions and even played for dancing at a ball.[18]

The Colonel loved a celebration and desired to "be in on everything". At the banquet honoring Hector Sproat for his rescue of Rodney Robinson from the river, Colonel Topping

[15] Trail Creek News, Feb. 12, 1897, Oct. 30, 1895, Feb. 8, 1896, Sept. 11, 1896, Aug. 12, 1898.
[16] Trail Creek News, April 2, 1897, April 9, 1897, May 7, 1897.
[17] Trail Creek News, May 23, 1896.
[18] Trail Creek News, April 9, 1897, June 25, 1897, Aug. 6, 1897.

acted as host. He presented a medal from the Royal Humane Society and kept up the spirits of the party with speech and song. "He rendered that beautiful ballad, 'The Old Clay Pipe', in a manner that nearly set fire to the house." [19]

On July 4, American Independence Day, Topping helped organize a day of sports and fun. High water prevented the ferry from running but the sternwheeler *Trail* carried crowds across the Columbia to see horse racing and a baseball game. At night dancing in the Hanna Block lasted until morning.[20]

August saw Trail's first wedding solemnized in the parlor of the Meakin Hotel when school principal Donald Dewar married Mrs. Edith Ellis of Waneta. Father Pat conducted the ceremony and "all were happy under the smile of Colonel Topping." [21]

Social life was gay. In summer there were fishing trips, hikes into the hills for flowers and huckleberries, excursions on the river. Sometimes the *Lytton* or the *Trail,* with flags flying and a band blaring music, carried holidayers to Deer Park for a day's picnic. On occasion a race between the two steamers enlivened proceedings. For a thrill, many people disembarked at Waterloo and returned downriver by rowboat or on a big raft of the B.C. Smelting & Refining Co. down the rapids at great speed. Riding and driving were popular. Colonel Topping owned a span of well-groomed handsome horses, and in his light buggy could make the long climb to Rossland in forty-four minutes.[22]

In winter fun moved indoors. All the churches held a variety of socials and concerts and a number of fraternal organizations appeared with their accompanying fellowship functions. The Maccabees formed Tent Number 5 late in 1896 while the Independent Order of Forresters soon followed suit and the Ancient Order of United Workmen established Lodge Number 9. In April 1897 the Knights of Pythias formed Trail Lodge

[19] Trail Creek News, May 29, 1896.
[20] Trail Creek News, July 10, 1896.
[21] Trail Creek News, Aug. 7, 1896.
[22] Trail Creek News, June 11, 1897.

Number 23. Membership flourished and the K.P.'s annual
ball was so popular it won for its sponsors the title of "princes
as entertainers". It was not until the fall of 1899 that local
Masons organized. On October 6, Fidelity Lodge Number 32
received its investiture charter. That same autumn the Odd-
fellows instituted Enterprise Lodge Number 43. Each of these
lodges held a Grand Ball, usually in the big frame Opera
House with its crenellated facade which stood on Cedar Avenue.
In addition there was the City Social Club which met weekly
for whist and dancing in the parlors of the Crown Point Hotel.

Many famous visitors passed through Trail on their way to
the Rossland mines, inspiring the cheerful newspaper to pithy
comment: "Trail is becoming a rendezvous for great men of
the world. The C.P.R. steamer *Kootenay* has worn out two
clothes-lines this year in running up flags in honor of distin-
guished men who have neglected their business affairs at home
long enough to pay Trail a visit." [23]

The only cloud in the Colonel's sky was a break in his
friendship with Frank Hanna. The two men had set up separate
real estate offices after their business dissolution in May. That
autumn Hanna inserted a notice in the local paper: "This is to
certify that I, the undersigned, will not be responsible for any
debts whatsoever contracted by Mrs. Jane Hanna in connection
with the support of my family and you will also take notice
that I am willing to support my own family under my own
management but not otherwise and have so stated and been
refused, hence this publication is made to guard myself and
guide others — Frank Hanna".[24]

The following spring Hanna affairs reached a climax when
Jane Hanna applied to the courts for an order making her
sole custodian of her children—a claim which was granted.[25]

As the year 1896 drew to its close, Christmas was celebrated
in churches bright with evergreens and decorations. Santa Claus
— often the Colonel in disguise — appeared at Christmas

[23] Trail Creek News, Oct. 22, 1897.
[24] Trail Creek News, Oct. 2, 1896.
[25] Rossland Miner, April 3, 1897, April 16, 1897.

Tree parties and presented gifts to starry-eyed children. It had been a good year and as the whistles of the smelter and the steamer *Lytton* joined in a shrill farewell on New Year's Eve, it passed out on a note of optimism. As Editor Thompson said: "Men are in Trail to-day in possession of competencies who one year ago were in red ink on the wrong side of life's financial column and none are here who are not better circumstanced than when 1896 opened for business in Trail." [26]

[26] Trail Creek News, Dec. 25, 1896.

4.

HARD TIMES IS THE CRY OF ALL

To AN ISOLATED camp like Rossland, transportation was very important. Heinze had furthered development of its undoubtedly rich mines by building the smelter and tramway to the Columbia River, but connection with the outside world was essential. He recognized the need and planned a railroad into the area. Others were aware of the same problem and the year 1897 was to see a struggle between rival railway companies, each striving to get control of access to the mines.

Daniel Chase Corbin of Spokane was one of the first to realize the potentiality of the Kootenays and he determined to run feeder lines from Spokane into all the mining camps. Having constructed the Spokane Falls and Northern Railway as far as Colville, he extended it to Northport in 1890, where connection was made with sternwheelers plying the Arrow Lakes. When gold was discovered along Kootenay Lake he obtained a charter to build the Nelson and Fort Sheppard branch from Northport to Nelson up the valley of Beaver Creek and the Salmon River. Here, at the base of mountains containing the Yankee Girl, Dundee and Ymir mines, he surveyed a townsite known as Quartz Creek, later called Ymir. Development of the Rossland mines encouraged him to build another extension up Sheep Creek to Rossland.

Known as the Red Mountain Railway it was completed by the end of 1896 and on a Sunday late in December Corbin and Chief Engineer Roberts went to Rossland for the official opening. Leaving the terminus on Nickel Plate Flat, the train ploughed through heavy snow with no difficulty, swung round the double loop near the O.K. mine, skirted Sheep Creek Canyon at a height of two hundred feet and reached Northport after an hour of travel. Crossing of the Columbia was by ferry but within the year a bridge was opened amid the tooting of whistles and the music of the Northport band. Corbin had provided complete rail service between Spokane and Rossland.[1]

At the same time the attention of the Canadian Pacific Railway Company was directed toward the Kootenay mines. In February 1897, by purchasing the Columbia and Kootenay Steam Navigation Company's fleet of sternwheelers, the C.P.R. gained control of transport on the Columbia River and Kootenay Lake.[2] During the summer it constructed a branch line through the Slocan valley and started work on an extension of the C.P.R. from Lethbridge to Nelson. Organized as the B.C. Southern, it would cross the Rockies through the Crow's Nest Pass. Valuable coal lands were obtained from the Dominion Government as part of its land grant. Not content with terminating the line at Kootenay Lake, Vice-President Shaughnessy, on a visit to Trail, said the C.P.R. definitely planned a connection into Rossland.[3]

Meanwhile Heinze was not idle. He envisioned a railroad between the Columbia valley and the Boundary country. For this purpose he organized the Columbia & Western Railway Company. He, his brother Arthur, Chester Glass of Spokane and F. E. Ward of Rossland were incorporators. Accompanied by Glass, Heinze sailed for England in the summer of 1896 to enlist capital for his enterprise. Upon his return he announced the C. & W.'s intention to construct a line along the Columbia River to Robson as the first step in his project.

[1] Trail Creek News, Dec. 25, 1896, April 30, Oct. 16, 1897.
[2] Trail Creek News, Dec. 25, 1896.
[3] Trail Creek News, June 4, Aug. 13, Aug. 27, 1897.

Contract for the work was given to Winters, Parsons and Boomer of Butte who arrived in the middle of winter with five carloads of supplies and thirty-one horses. Camps were set up at Rock Creek, Blueberry Creek and Boomer's Landing near Waterloo. By summer all grading was done and the bridges completed, including the high trestle over Stoney Creek. The work of laying rails proceeded rapidly and in late September of 1897 an engine whistle echoing from Smelter Hill signified junction with the narrow-gauge tramway to Rossland. Many people from Trail climbed the hill to see the driving of the last spike while a crew of men followed the engine, surfacing and ballasting the track. Twenty-one miles long, the railway made connection at Robson with the C.P.R.'s Columbia & Kootenay branch by means of a ferry crossing. On the Trail side of the Columbia a new townsite was surveyed on land owned by McLeary and Heinze and was given the name of Castlegar.[4]

With connection between the lake boats and the Rossland mines now established, Heinze sought a charter and subsidy for an extension over the mountains to the Boundary country. Here he encountered opposition both from Corbin, who planned a feeder line up the Kettle River, and from the C.P.R., whose interest in the Kootenays was increasing.

Corbin, shrewd manipulator that he was, entered the fray using other tactics than railroad construction. In the summer of 1897 Heinze's contract with the LeRoi Company for ore was due to expire, so Corbin offered the mine owners a one-third interest in the townsite of Northport and lower freight rates if they would build a smelter at that town. The proposition was accepted and in August James Breen, who had designed the B.C.S.& R. smelter, began construction of a plant at Northport. Herman C. Bellinger was lured away from Heinze to become its general manager and many workmen followed him to work in the American town.

Citizens of Trail and Rossland were appalled at the turn

[4] Trail Creek News, March 21, 1896, Jan. 8, 1897, Sept. 24, 1897, Oct. 1, 1897, Oct. 16, 1897.

of events. Indignation meetings demanded an export duty on lead ores. Topping expressed popular opinion when he stated that while the American owners of the LeRoi had developed the mine they owed something to the country where they had become rich. Local newspapers attacked the projected smelter and the Trail Creek News coined the slogan, "Canadian Ores for Canadian Smelters".[5]

There is no doubt the building of the Northport smelter was a serious blow to Heinze who admitted that the entire output of the Rossland mines, aside from the LeRoi, would not keep a fair-sized smelter in operation. Nevertheless, he erected a mess house and an assay office in Trail and in August produced the first gold brick ever refined in Canada. Weighing twenty-one pounds, it was stamped with the initials, B.C.S.& R. Co., and was placed on display in the Bank of Montreal in Rossland.[6]

Heinze encountered other opponents when he applied to the Railway Committee of the Dominion Parliament for a subsidy for his proposed railroad to Penticton. Opposition appeared from a group of financiers who had organized the Victoria, Vancouver and Eastern Railway Company to build from the Coast to the Okanagan. Owing to the dispute, the Railway Committee refused to grant a subsidy to anyone. At once a hue and cry arose in the towns of British Columbia and more indignation meetings were held, protesting the government's action. In Trail, Colonel Topping addressed a group in plain language, attacking those interests which he called "charter-mongering promoters", and demanding a subsidy for Heinze's Columbia and Western.

Late in the summer Heinze returned to Trail, disappointed at the turn of events. In a statement he said, "I have done more for this part of the country than all the others put together. I have never been sparing of money when development demanded and I consider it would have been but just had my efforts been appreciated and the road to Penticton subsidized.

[5] Trail Creek News, July 16, 1897, Aug. 6, 1897, April 16, 1897.
[6] Trail Creek News, Aug. 13, 1897.

In October the promoters of the V.V.&E. sold the controlling interest in their charter to Mackenzie and Mann, contractors who were building the B.C. Southern for the C.P.R. It was now evident that the C.P.R. was determined to obtain access to the Kootenay mines.

As the year drew to its close rumor was rife that Heinze was dickering for the sale of his smelter and rail lines. Late in December he and Carlos Warfield registered in a Montreal hotel and many conficting statements appeared in news dispatches. Reports of a sale were followed by denials, but finally in February, 1898, Vice-President Shaughnessy announced that the C.P.R. had acquired the property of the British Columbia Smelting and Refining Company. The price of purchase was a cause of much speculation. Some newspapers claimed Heinze had asked and received one million dollars, but the general opinion favored the sum of eight hundred thousand — two hundred thousand for the smelter and six hundred thousand for the railway between Trail and Robson and the narrow-gauge to Rossland. Heinze retained his sawmill, his interest in the Trail and Robson townsites, logging camps upriver and one-half of the railway land grant.

Leaving D. J. Fitzgerald to supervise his interests in Trail, Heinze returned to Butte, Montana, where he became involved in fantastic lawsuits against his rivals in the copper industry. For several years the litigants fought each other with chicanery, bribery, besmirching of the law courts and even bloodshed until in 1906 Heinze sold his interests to his competitors for a reputed ten million dollars. He then established a chain of banks in New York but sudden failure precipitated an investigation which resulted in his indictment for breach of the Banking Act. He was acquitted but his power was broken and his spectacular career at an end.

All this was still in the future as the high-living, personable young Heinze — he was not yet thirty — passed from the Kootenay area. Like some brilliant bird of passage, he had alighted briefly in the alien pine forests and rocky outcrops of southern British Columbia, bringing the glamor of prosperity

and promise of wealth. The promise was shortlived and seemed
to perish at his going, but the editor of the Trail Creek News
could not let him leave without a farewell salute: "He is of
the stamp of western hustlers that never quit until they have
won and to whom nothing seems impossible. To him Trail
owes all. A dozen men such as Mr. Heinze working together
to the same end could pick up B.C. and in one year push it
higher than it has climbed in the last decade." [7]

The last months of 1897 were full of gloom for the little
settlement of Trail. Erection of the Northport smelter took many
workmen from the plant while withdrawal of LeRoi ore reduced its operations. Heinze's failure to obtain a railway subsidy brought uncertainty and the town's optimism oozed
rapidly. Businessmen felt the pinch of falling sales and hard
luck was the cry of all. W. K. Esling, who had started a
real estate and loan business, sold to James Worth and planned
a return to the Coast to do newspaper work. The Kootenay
brewery was sold at auction by the sheriff.

News of the purchase of the smelter by the Canadian Pacific
Railway did not improve matters. The new owners closed the
smelter temporarily but seemed in no hurry to re-open. Editor
Thompson of the Trail Creek News had always been a great
supporter of Heinze but he made an effort to reassure the
townspeople about the C.P.R. and called on them for patience
during the takeover period. After a visit to the smelter he was
impressed by the new manager, Walter Hull Aldridge, and reported: "He is a man of the world, an affable gentleman and
has the air of one thoroughly conversant with the business he
has in hand. The News at least will not attempt to give him any
advice as to how he should conduct his company's affairs but is
confident that under his management Trail smelter will start
up again at the earliest possible moment and be run with as
great success as heretofore." [8]

[7] Trail Creek News, June 18, 1897, June 25, 1897, July 16, 1897, Oct. 16,
1897, Dec. 10, 1897, Dec. 17, 1897, Jan. 29, 1898, Feb. 4, 1898, Feb.
12, 1898, Feb. 26, 1898.
[8] Trail Creek News, March 12, 1898.

Despite the optimism of his sentiments, Thompson saw no future for himself in Trail and in April he disposed of his interest in the Trail Creek News to Esling and Blackmer. He set off for Glenora in the new Stikine-Yukon gold excitement planning to edit the Glenora Daily News. To an idle smelter town the Klondike goldfields presented great contrast and the effervescent Thompson saw them in a rosy glow.

"Trail has a Klondike route," he wrote. "Up the road to Rossland and then downhill to Northport. From Northport to Marcus, the roads are perfect and from Marcus to Ashcroft you have your choice of any trail you may find. From Ashcroft to Glenora the road is macadamized and shade trees are to be found at intervals along the route. At Glenora you visit the Glenora Daily News office for further instructions and late exchanges. All voyageurs from Trail will feel at home in Glenora news office for a Trail man prints the paper. From Glenora to Klondike is a summer day's picnic." [9]

So flitted from Trail the "irrepressible, flowery-penned newsman the rustler, eighteen carats fine", W. F. Thompson. Hailed as one of the pioneers who had helped build Trail, he left the log cabin on Spokane street, mute evidence, with its erratically designed cupola and bear den, of his imagination and originality.

Entrance of the C.P.R. seemed to spark other changes in the Trail Creek area. Within the year Corbin would sell his railway interests to the Northern Pacific (later it was acquired by the Great Northern) while the Spokane capitalists who had developed the mines on Red Mountain withdrew from the district.

Patrick Clark and his associates had already disposed of the War Eagle to the Toronto syndicate of Gooderham and Blackstock in 1896. In April 1898, Gooderham and Blackstock also bought the Centre Star at a price of two million dollars, and at the same time the LeRoi Company placed its property on the market. During negotiations a rift developed which led to involved litigation.

[9] Trail Creek News, April 9, April 30, 1898.

To effect a sale of the LeRoi Colonel Peyton journeyed to Europe, offering the mine at a price of three million dollars. He found a buyer in the British American Corporation, a company organized by Whittaker Wright and the Honorable Charles Mackintosh, formerly Lieutenant-Governor of the North West Territories. An agreement of sale was signed in London but later at the ensuing meeting of shareholders a minority group led by Judge George Turner, Colonel W. W. Turner and mine manager W. J. Harris objected to the price and refused to surrender their shares. However, the majority group lodged 262,000 shares in the Bank of British North America in Rossland as escrow and accepted five hundred thousand dollars in immediate payment. The sum of one million, forty-two thousand and fifty-four dollars remained to be paid.

The dispute between the two groups concerned the interpretation of British and American law. The British American Corporation contended that as the majority shareholder it was entitled to operate the mine. The minority group insisted that as the company was registered in the State of Washington it was not subject to British law and that since no alien could hold property in Washington the B.A.C. could not run the Northport smelter. Secretary Williams of the LeRoi Company feared the Turner (minority) group might try to impound company documents so he gathered them together and took them from Spokane to Rossland, only to find he had been forestalled by the substitution of another seal in place of that belonging to the LeRoi Company. The B.A.C. and the majority group were rendered powerless to transact any legal business.

Carrying the fight further, the Turner group obtained an injunction prohibiting members of the opposition from leaving the United States. To enforce the order, deputies were hired to stop all trains to Canada from Spokane. Mackintosh countered this move by hiring a special coach from Austin Corbin, president of the Red Mountain Railway, and placed three important shareholders aboard. The train engineer was commanded to stop for nothing until the border was crossed. When Mackintosh and his party entered the train Sheriff Bunce tried to prevent them from leaving Spokane but on the personal intervention of Austin Corbin the train left the station. However, the sheriff held a gun on the crew and remained in the coach until Northport was reached. There he was persuaded to leave, on threat of arrest in Canada for carrying a deadly weapon. Arrived in Rossland, Mackintosh applied to the County Court to place the LeRoi mine in receivership. This was done. W. J. Harris was ousted as manager and W. A. Carlyle was appointed receiver. He immediately cut production to a minimum. Feelings had been bitter between the groups as Harris was accused of gutting the mine by shipping as much ore as possible to Northport to remove it from Canadian jurisdiction. However, the receivership was set aside and Billy Harris returned as mine manager. Shipments continued to Northport.

The minority group now applied to the Superior Court of the State of Washington for an injunction restraining the B.A.C. from taking possession of the LeRoi stock being held in escrow in the Bank of British North America in Rossland. Mackintosh countered by announcing that the B.A.C. assigned all its rights to shares of the LeRoi Company to the Corporation's assignee who was represented by the Bank of Montreal in Rossland. J. S. C. Fraser, manager of the Bank of Montreal then wrote the manager of the Bank of British North America advising that he had been instructed to pay the Bank of B.N.A. the sum of one million, forty-two thousand and fifty-four dollars and take delivery of LeRoi shares. He enclosed the cheque signed by C. H. Mackintosh, received the shares for B.A.C.

Turner made one last play by announcing a new company was to take over the minority group's shares but late in November a settlement was reached at a compromise price. The remaining stock was handed over to the British American Corporation who thus became complete owners of the LeRoi property. Spokane financeers withdrew from Rossland, no longer in control but well rewarded for their efforts.

Within a period of eighteen months, British and Canadian businessmen had invested eleven million dollars in the Trail Creek area and were to dominate its development in the future.

5.

THE TIDE BEGINS TO TURN

Walter Hull Aldridge, appointed by the Canadian Pacific Railway Company to manage its newly acquired smelter, had been born in Brooklyn on September 8, 1867. After graduating from the Columbia School of Mines in 1887, he worked five years as assayer, chemist and metallurgist in Colorado. He was manager of the Great Falls and Helena plants of the United States Smelting & Refining Company when Sir William Van Horne asked him to organize the mining and metallurgical interests of the C.P.R. Intrigued by the proposition, Aldridge accepted and came to Trail to take charge of the Canadian Smelting Works.[1] Its former owner, F. Augustus Heinze, had been a fellow student at the Columbia School of Mines and to the young Aldridge there was a challenge in following a man whose weaknesses he knew as well as his qualities of brilliance. The two men were worlds apart in temperament, the one a gambler of questionable honesty and the other, an administrator, straightforward and thoroughly reliable.

Aldridge again met Heinze, this time before the terms of sale with the C.P.R. had been arranged. He had come to Trail to value the smelter but could not agree with Heinze's

[1] Trail Daily Times, Aug. 12, 1959.

estimate. To break the stalemate, Aldridge suggested an adjudicator and J. S. C. Fraser, Manager of the Bank of Montreal, was agreed upon. Although it was late at night, the two men bundled themselves into a sleigh, roused Fraser from sleep and put the case before him. Fraser awarded two points to Heinze and one to Aldridge but the latter considered his the important concession, so agreement was reached.

Now in the spring of '98, with the plant shut down, Aldridge planned its revision. After taking an inventory, he announced that one hundred thousand dollars would be spent on improvements. New copper blast furnaces would be added and two lead furnaces built to handle the silver-lead ores from the Slocan. To replace open-air roasting, ovens or stalls would be built and the fumes carried away in big stacks. The whole plant was to be operated by electricity. Heinze had used steam, burning cordwood for fuel, and had supplemented this with a small amount of electricity from the power station he built at the foot of Smelter Hill on Pine Avenue. During the summer of 1898 Sir Charles Ross and the owners of the Centre Star mine had formed the West Kootenay Power and Light Company to generate power for the Rossland mines from the Middle Falls of the Kootenay River. A powerhouse was constructed at Bonnington and a transmission line was laid into Rossland to a substation on the Idaho claim. Aldridge now planned to tap this line near Murphy Creek and run a branch to a substation in the smelter yards. Electricity would thus come from both the Bonnington plant and the little Trail powerhouse. As time went on, the Bonnington station was enlarged to supply all the electricity needed for mines, smelter and the town of Trail.[2]

Work on the smelter revision began in May as Sol Cameron started excavation and the moulding of two million bricks required for chimney stacks and forty-eight roast stalls. Soon ore was again shipped from the War Eagle, Centre Star, and Iron Mask and piled in the smelter yard. In the summer five

[2] Trail Creek News, April 23, May 6, 1898, April 12, 1897, April 9, 1897.

roast heaps were fired and many workmen who had gone to the Northport smelter the preceding year returned to Trail. On a Sunday morning in August the Canadian Smelting Works blew in its copper furnaces and the plant was again in operation.

The townspeople were delighted and regarded the disagreeable sulphur fumes as welcome evidence of the return of prosperous times. Work continued on the sampling mill for lead ore, on the lead furnaces, and on the Bruckner roasters. The entire plant was roofed with corrugated iron and very little of Heinze's smelter was left — just the old stack which was used for the lead furnaces. The new stack for the copper roast stalls, one hundred and seventy-five feet in height, was completed in December and in honor of the event the brick-masons raised four flags from its top — three Union Jacks and one Stars and Stripes! [3]

Eighteen ninety-eight was a year of great railway building activity. With the purchase of Heinze's property, the C.P.R. acquired his charter for a line from Robson to Midway but had no subsidy. At the same time Corbin was asking for a charter for a branch line from Northport to Cascade up the Kettle Valley. Spokane interests favored him, as did Rossland. Van Horne and Shaughnessy opposed the application, pointing out that Corbin had done nothing to develop Canada, all his interests being centred in Spokane and in the diversion of ore to the United States. In April an Ottawa report declared that Corbin's charter had been granted and American newspapers ran big headlines of jubilation while the Northport band turned out to celebrate. However the triumph was premature. Corbin had received approval merely from the Railway Committee and not from the House of Commons. The Trail Creek News stated its position unequivocally: "We are glad the Americans rejoiced prematurely. There can be no doubt as to Trail's position in the matter of American railroad builders. Trail is in Canada and all its interests are Canadian. Without protection our town cannot endure. Trail is a smelter town

[3] Trail Creek News, May 6, 1898, Jan. 6, April 8, April 15, Sept. 2.

and needs Canadian ores to keep its smelter in operation. So far as it lies in its power, Trail will continue to work for the defeat of any measure that has for its purpose the securing of Canadian ores for American smelters or Canadian patronage for American merchants."

Corbin failed to get his charter. In May a subsidy was granted to the C.P.R. and tenders were immediately called for construction of a line from Robson to Midway.[4]

Construction of this line was an epic achievement. Using horses, scrapers, shovels and manpower, contractors Mann, Larsen and Foley cut a grade around the precipitous bluffs of the Arrow Lake, up the steep pass at the headwaters of Dog Creek and down McRae Creek valley to Christina Lake. Superintending the work was William Francis Tye, the burly six-foot-four Chief Engineer for the C.P.R. and his assistant, John G. Sullivan. Both men were about thirty-five years of age and in the prime of life. They had need of health for their job was not an easy one.

Early in the year, while snow still lay thick on the hills, survey parties had explored the pass over the mountains between Arrow and Christina lakes, in preparation for the cutting of a tote road. Headquarters for construction was set up at Brooklyn, a gentle slope fanning out in the Arrow Lake three miles below the mouth of Dog Creek. Here a wharf was built and warehouses erected. Sternwheelers called daily to unload food, horses, two-wheeled carts, blasting powder, hoisting engines and all necessary supplies.

Brooklyn had belonged to a prospector named William Parker whose luck in finding mines had been negligible. Now, with the coming of the railway builders, he struck it rich. Firstcomers pitched tents or slept in blankets under the trees, but soon a townsite was laid out and lots sold for fifty dollars and quickly rose to two hundred. John Petersen of the Crown Point Hotel in Trail built a second Crown Point beside the creek and in a month's time was serving meals continuously

[4] Trail Creek News, April 9, 1898, May 13, 1898.

from five A.M. until long after nightfall. Other hotels appeared and Trail businessmen erected stores on the flat above the lake. A few houses and a hospital were built. Pat Burns, who contracted to supply meat to the railway crews, set up a slaughter house beyond the town and drove hundreds of cattle over the road to Cascade. Five days after its beginning the settlement boasted a newspaper, printed in Trail by Esling and Blackmer and distributed among the workmen. Hectic life had suddenly come to Brooklyn.

From Robson the railway hugged the shore between mountains and lake for several miles but soon had to angle up the hillside until at Brooklyn it was one thousand feet above the town. Tunnels were driven through cliffs rising sheer from the lake and at the height of land a tunnel three thousand feet in length was pushed through the rock. It took one year to cut this tunnel using the only power drill on the line. So much tunnelling demanded large quantities of blasting powder and many explosions were terrific in size. Reverberations echoed round the hills; huge trees were uprooted and the place looked like a wheat field after hail. As the line wound its way into the mountains it had to cross dozens of creeks and gulleys which required bridging. The biggest bridge spanned the Kettle River near Cascade City and was one thousand feet long and one hundred and eighty feet high.

With the progression of the line other towns had a brief but brilliant life. Gladstone, in the McRae Creek valley, was headquarters for timbering and a freighting centre, while at the foot of Christina Lake the town of Minto appeared in October, 1898. Near the tunnels on Eholt Pass, Niagara boomed with a population rising from zero to six hundred.

One year after the beginning of construction the first locomotive crossed the Kettle River bridge and by November the line reached Greenwood. Early in December of 1899 an excursion party of one hundred and fifty businessmen and officials travelled over the new road, revelling in its spectacular scenery. At Greenwood they were met by a brass band and driven by hack to a celebration banquet. They lustily toasted the Queen, the Board of Trade and the C.P.R. and were loud in their praise of the railway company for completing the gigantic project. It had cost fifty thousand dollars per mile but everyone thought it was well worth it. The mines of Deadwood Camp, of Phoenix, of Rossland and the smelters at Trail, Grand Forks and Greenwood now had an outlet to the markets of the world.

What of the boom towns which flourished during construction? A devastating fire swept Cascade in September, 1899, wiping out its central block of hotels. Gladstone, Minto and Niagara just disappeared. As for Brooklyn, it had passed out of existence before the railway was completed. As the line moved westward, its buildings had been stripped of windows and doors by hotelmen who followed the work crews. In September, 1899, Brooklyn was burned to ashes and a visitor to the place "went to the spot where the town had been and then almost wondered if he had dreamed of there having been such a place." Its life cycle was complete and Billy Parker's claim reverted to the solitary forest as it was before the eventful year of 1898. Rumor had it that after the railway was finished, Parker himself was as poor as he had been before.[5]

In the summer of 1898 the C.P.R. began widening the narrow-gauge line between Trail and Rossland. Trains were run only at night so work could progress during the day. Winter snows forced stoppage of rail laying but it was resumed the following spring and in mid-June, 1899, the gaily decorated engine of the first standard-gauge train left Smelter Junction and pulled into Rossland forty minutes later. The old narrow-gauge had passed into history.[6]

Meanwhile, late in '98, the C.P.R. finished its B.C. Southern line through the Crow's Nest Pass from Lethbridge to Kushanook and wishing to celebrate the occasion invited one hundred

[5] Trail Creek News, June 3, 1898, June 17, June 24, 1898, Sept. 30, Sept. 2, Oct. 17, Nov. 14, Dec. 2, 1898, Aug. 19, 1899, Sept. 19, Nov. 11, 1899.
Rossland Record, Dec. 11, 1899.
[6] Trail Creek News, June 17, 1899, July 15, July 22, 1898.

local businessmen on an excursion over the new road. From Trail came Colonel Topping, R. T. Daniel, Jim Worth, D. J. Dewar, Dr. Corsan and Superintendent Gutelius. Boarding the sternwheeler *Moyie* at Nelson, they steamed up the lake to Kootenay Landing. Here a special train with three sleeping cars carried them to Cranbrook which they reached in time to attend a banquet. The next morning they went on to Fernie and inspected the coal mines and coke ovens of the Crow's Nest Pass Coal Company. Returning to Cranbrook they left the train to drive in sleighs through a clear frosty night to Fort Steele where the Board of Trade and a brass band welcomed them to another banquet. After pausing at Moyie to inspect the St. Eugene and Moyie mines, they returned to Nelson and a final banquet where the grateful excursionists showed their appreciation by the presentation of gifts to C.P.R. officials — a sterling silver tea-set, a piano lamp, tobacco jar, silver match box and silver flask. Colonel Topping, one of the speakers, was loud in his praise of the new railroad.[7]

All this railway construction, followed by the re-opening of the smelter, brought an upsurge of business in Trail during late 1898 and '99. After months of stagnation the Canadian Mutual Loan & Investment Company of Toronto notified James Worth that it was ready to lend money again for use in Trail. Some storekeepers set up shops in Brooklyn to supply railway workmen while others engaged in the freighting business. R. T. Daniel, ever a man with an eye for profit, put four-horse teams on the road from Bossburg to Cascade, Grand Forks and Greenwood, carrying supplies for the railroad. James Worth bought an interest in a livery stable and later set up a chicken ranch at Deer Park to provide work camps with poultry. Clark and Binns, furniture dealers, established a branch store in Phoenix to sell iron bedsteads, mattresses and springs for the bunkhouses of Knob Hill and Ironside mines. W. K. Esling continued to publish the Trail Creek News.

[7] Trail Creek News, Dec. 9, 1898, Dec. 16, 1898.

Fire protection for the town was improved by the erection of a wooden firehall on the corner of Eldorado street where the railway trestle crossed Bay Avenue Bridge. A fifty-foot tower rose above a meeting room and verandahed bandstand, while storage space for two hose reel carts was provided. Topping was elected president of the fire brigade whose uniforms of white shirts and black trousers were made by Mrs. Heard. The Chief bought caps for the boys and rubber coats and boots were purchased. The fire teams practised regularly and appeared in hose reel contests at all celebrations.[8]

To Colonel Topping the town's progress was all-important but he also concerned himself with the affairs of smelter, railroads and politics and he expressed opinions on every question. Never one to mince words, he used forthright language such as the time he protested the practice of the government of "inflicting upon many parts of the country fossils from the Cariboo to fill important offices where brains and courtesy are required and where men are needed who can tell a mine from a cow without the latter being belled."

He spoke at public gatherings, wrote letters to the newspaper and in March '98 formed a Board of Trade to protest the granting of a charter to Corbin and to ask for the placing of a duty on lead. The Board requested money from the provincial government to improve the town's streets and clear its alleys of shacks and outbuildings, and to build a wagon road up Lookout Mountain to the mines. R. T. Daniel made a special trip to Victoria and secured four thousand dollars for the Lookout road. Starting at the brewery, it was built up the hillside to the school and then angled up the slope to terminate on the April Fool ground, just below the gap between the two peaks. To Topping and Daniel this road seemed essential, for to them "Lookout was that great peak which is destined to become one of the greatest ore producing mountains in the West Kootenay."[9]

[8] Trail Creek News, May 6, 1898, Jan. 6, April 8, April 15, Sept. 2, Sept. 9, Aug. 26, Nov. 11, 1899, May 20, June 25, Sept. 16, 1898.
[9] March 26, Sept. 9, April 30, 1898.

The personal life of the Colonel was decidedly irregular. He still resided in the Hanna cottage although Frank Hanna was rarely in town and spent much of his time prospecting and returned to Trail only to oversee his property. Jane Hanna looked for support and help to "Toppins" as she called the Colonel. In the summer of '98 she and her five children contracted measles and when hot weather enveloped the town in a blanket, Topping and Jim Worth took the family to Deer Park to camp on the beach. They travelled upriver in the Colonel's newly purchased launch, the *Oriole,* a small wood-burning vessel capable of carrying ten persons. Jim Worth, the big, blonde, good-looking nephew of Topping, acted as skipper and piloted the Hanna girls on many pleasant outings during the summer.

As the year wore on into fall and winter Jim and seventeen-year old Maud Hanna fell in love and the following spring they were married. Father Pat performed the ceremony in the flower-decked parlor of the Hanna home. Maud chose a tailor-made gown, light fawn in color. After honeymooning in Spokane the young couple began their married life in a house donated by Jane and furnished by Colonel Topping.

Late summer saw another wedding in the Hanna family. Ollie married Herb Lewis, the banjo-playing deputy postmaster. Gowned in white swiss over blue silk with trimmings of lace and ribbon, Ollie was attended by her sister Sophie, while Rev. Calvert of the Methodist Church performed the ceremony. The Lewises took up residence on Spokane Street in a house behind the Meakin Hotel.[10]

Romance seemed to bloom in Trail that year of 1899. In January the young manager of the Canadian Smelting Works, Walter Aldridge, married Nancy Elnorah Tuttle, daughter of Dr. and Mrs. Jay Tuttle of Rossland. The wedding was a gala affair with guests from Trail, Northport and Nelson overflowing Rossland's St. George's church. The bride, wearing a brown travelling dress, was gracious, dignified and very lovely.

[10] Trail Creek News, July 15, 1898, Aug. 26, 1899, March 11, 1899, Aug. 19, 1899.

Her sister Nettie acted as bridesmaid while the groomsman was J. S. C. Fraser, manager of the Bank of Montreal. At the conclusion of the ceremony the Rev. Henry Irwin (Father Pat) blessed the couple after a quaint custom of the Old Country by tying with his stole a true-love knot around their clasped hands. Then speeding over the crisp snow by sleigh, the newly-weds boarded the Spokane train for a honeymoon in San Francisco. On their return they began married life in the handsome new house, "Holly Fern Place", built beyond the smelter on the high bluff above the Columbia River. Gifts were many and included an eight-foot hall clock of polished oak, given by smelter employees.

6.

TRIUMPH FOR THE COLONEL

THE YEAR 1900 continued to involve Topping in a whirl of activity. Concerned as he was with the baseball team, the brass band, the fire brigade, the waterworks and numerous banquets, he found time for still another enterprise. On a March evening he presided at a meeting of men interested in forming a Rifle corps. Upon the suggestion of a young mining engineer from the smelter, Selwyn Gwillim Blaylock, the name Trail Rifle Association was adopted. Customs Collector D. B. Stevens was elected president and a schedule of weekly drills was planned until guns could be secured from the Militia Department. Colonel Topping closed the meeting with a speech in which he regretted that he was too old to drill. He stated that although he had been born under another flag and had seen active service in another country he possessed a warm spot in his heart for the Union Jack and would do all he could to further the association's success.[1]

A few days later Topping left Trail to visit his home in New York which he had not seen for thirty-three years. There he was re-united with his sisters, Mrs. Agnes Stiles and Jim Worth's mother, Mrs. Lydia Worth. Returning as a successful man he was hailed as the poor boy who left home to fight in

[1] Trail Creek News, March 3, 1900.

the Indian wars and was now one of the richest men in British Columbia. On his way back to Trail by train he had a disturbing experience. He was suddenly awakened at night by extreme difficulty in breathing. The pain was severe but was relieved by a fellow passenger who rubbed his chest for several hours. However, it was some time after his return home before he recovered from the effects of the congestion.[2]

In May, fire destroyed the home of the Lewises. Herb had a toothache one night and after building a good fire in the stove, went to bed. He was awakened about half-past one by flames enveloping the house. Ollie Lewis and her sister-in-law escaped in their nightgowns. The clanging firebell and the baying of Chief Devitt's bloodhound roused the firemen who arrived quickly, but a hose pipe burst and although an iron collar was secured over the break the nozzle was jammed by a piece of wood. By then the blaze had made so much headway it was impossible to save the house or any of its contents.[3]

That autumn tragedy struck Jane Hanna's family again. Her daughter Maud, the young wife of Jim Worth, died giving birth to a son. The whole community was shocked and on the day of the funeral all stores closed while the town fire bell sounded a dirge. Maud was buried in the cemetery on Smelter Flats beside her brother Frankie and a memorial service was held in St. Andrew's Church. Jane undertook the care of the baby.[4]

Mining promotion still occupied much of the Colonel's time. He was always looking for another LeRoi and wherever a new field opened, he bought claims, sometimes for re-sale, often for himself. In the Lardeau he secured the Ethel group and succeeded in interesting Spokane money in them. He also acquired an interest in the British Chief at the head of Beaver Creek and in a property near Nelson on Bird Creek. Late in '98 he and the Petersen brothers sold the townsite of Deer

[2] Trail Creek News, March 10, July 7, 1900. May 12, 1900.
  Rossland Record, March 28, 1900.
[3] Trail Creek News, May 12, 1900.
[4] Trail Creek News, Sept. 15, 1900.

Park to Governor Mackintosh but retained their mining claims in the hills above the town.

However, the prospects on Lookout Mountain were his special concern. Owning the Blue Chip, Little Giant, Gray Cliff and St. Croix, he was also president of the Little Joe Mining Company and a director of the Wolverine Gold Mining Company. He always said that one paying property on Lookout was all that was needed for a boom. In the spring of 1900 it seemed as if his wish might be granted when an English syndicate started work on the Little Giant. Much stir was caused in Trail when seven packhorses laden with supplies prepared to climb the hillside to the mine. They carried sections of a whin which the manager planned to use for removing rock from a shaft. The whin was to be driven by horses who could feed on the high grass covering the bowl-like depression where the mine lay. However, the project came to nothing and when work stopped for the winter it was not resumed.[5]

One of Colonel Topping's brightest prospects was in the State of Washington, on Toroda Creek. Here in what was known as Sheridan Camp, he and Dave Snyder acquired the Zala M. and the Fanny Woodward. Convinced that these mines would prove very rich, he planned installation of a reduction works. He was also attracted to mines in Sumpter camp in the northeastern part of Oregon and according to reports sank eighty thousand dollars in various properties.[6]

As early as the spring of 1897 Colonel Topping had identified himself with a move for the incorporation of Trail as a city and had declared that the settlement could not progress but would drift, listless and indifferent, until clothed with responsibility. Now this became one of his chief interests. He was strongly supported by the editor of the Trail Creek News, William K. Esling, whose opinion was that "the sooner we break loose from this cheese-paring, thin-skinned government

[5] Trail Creek News, Aug. 20, 1897, Sept. 16, 1898, March 18, May 13, 1899, May 23, 1896, Oct. 8, 1897, Feb. 12, 1898, Aug. 4, 1900. Sept. 1, 1900, Oct. 20, 1900.
[6] Trail Creek News, June 24, 1899, July 29, 1899.

and run our own municipal affairs, the better for us." Esling criticized businessmen for lack of initiative, scathingly writing, "Wanted — for the town of Trail, a little public spirit." He recalled Trail as it had been three years previously. "Three years ago we lived on what we made by our industry and thrift; now we are more predatory and live upon each other. Then we were busy and amiable; now we are idle and irascible. Let the citizens conserve energies, incorporate and work for the good of the town." [7]

In mid-December of 1900 a large mass meeting, sponsored by the Board of Trade, discussed the question of incorporation. Some people thought the move would entail further taxes without results equal to the cost but the majority favored it. They eyed the large license fees collected by the government, and the meagre grants received in return. Colonel Topping suggested a letter be sent to large property owners asking their opinion. Accordingly, a letter was sent to W. H. Aldridge of the Canadian Smelting Works, Richard Marpole of the C.P.R. and R. T. Daniel of Spokane, itemizing expenses and resources —

"Expenses would be as follows:
"City Clerk to act as assessor, collector and chief of police

Salary per annum (say)	$1200.00
Night police (say)	900.00
Rent and light of city hall	300.00
	$2400.00

"To meet this we have:

14 hotel licences at $200 per year	$2800.00
48 trades' licenses at $10	480.00
Real property tax	1500.00
Police court fines	500.00
	$5280.00

"Thus giving the city $2880.00 to spend in local improvements.

[7] Trail Creek News, March 26, 1898, Feb. 11, Feb. 18, Mar. 18, 1899.

We would not include Smelter Hill in the area for incorporation unless the companies owning the property request it.

> D. B. Stevens, Chairman,
> Incorporation Committee." [8]

Replies favored incorporation.

Meanwhile the Board of Trade under President Topping continued to hold meetings to study the necessary requirements for incorporation. To strengthen its powers it decided to become a registered society and on December 11, 1900, it was recorded in the department of the Secretary of State for Canada as the "Trail Board of Trade." E. H. Lewis was declared its secretary and the town's population was stated as being not less than twenty-five hundred.

The movement for incorporation had now gained so much momentum that a committee consisting of D. B. Stevens, E. S. Topping, George Weir, M. Blake and A. B. McKenzie was appointed to take the required steps. They retained John S. Clute as solicitor to present the petition to the legislature while J. D. Anderson surveyed the proposed corporation limits. These included the original Topping pre-emption plus a block one-half mile by one mile on the west and a block one-quarter mile square on the east. After several months of work details were completed and on June 14, 1901, Lieutenant-Governor Henri Joli de Lotbinière signed the letters patent establishing the corporation of the City of Trail.

On June 29, a group of citizens of the new city gathered in the big, barnlike Brown's Hall on Spokane street to nominate candidates for the offices of Mayor and Aldermen. E. S. Topping was the unanimous choice for Mayor but nine men were nominated for the six aldermanic posts. On July 6, elections were held and one hundred and nineteen of the one hundred and forty-three registered voters cast their ballots for a Council consisting of James Paterson Byers, Charles Atkinson McAnally, William John Furnell, James Dawson, Noble Binns and Alexander E. Steele. It was a proud day for the Colonel.

[8] Trail Creek News, Dec. 15, 1900, Dec. 29, 1900.

Ever since the time ten years before when he stepped ashore to a tenantless forest he had envisioned a flourishing town at the mouth of Trail Creek. Now it was an actuality and he had the honor of being the first Mayor. Unofficially known as the Father of Trail, he was now its leading citizen.[9]

Dominion Day, July 1st was chosen to be Inauguration Day for the new city. Committees had been at work for several weeks and had collected over seven hundred dollars, so everything favored a gala celebration. The day dawned bright and clear after two months of rain and spread a glow over the gay streamers, flags and evergreen decorations hanging from every store front. Hundreds of people thronged the streets and early in the morning the first train from Rossland chugged into town, loaded to capacity. Many people followed in carriages, by horseback or walking. From his home on the far side of the Columbia came Indian Joe and all day long he was seen on the streets, riding his horse and leading a couple of others.

Baseball, lacrosse and children's races filled the morning while at noon a Calathumpian Parade marched along the big bridge. Led by Chief of Police Devitt on a gray charger, it was made up of decorated carriages, school children waving flags, four veterans just returned from the Boer War, and two brass bands. The crowd was convulsed by P. Burns & Co.'s float depicting a sausage factory. As a crank was turned, dogs, cats and boys were thrown into a huge machine which spewed out sausages. Bringing up the rear the fire brigade hove into sight. Suddenly smoke appeared from a shack on Spokane street and the firemen rushed to quench it with a garden hose. Yanking out a smoking bed tick and a keg of beer they "tapped the beer and proceeded to extinguish their thirst, unmindful of the burning mattress."

The crowd in high good humor after the parade, surged toward the river to watch swimming, diving and tub races. Then they returned to the ball grounds to cheer Austrians or

[9] Trail Creek News, Dec. 22, 1900, Feb. 16, March 9, May 18, June 22, June 29, 1901.

Italians in a tug-of-war, to watch running events and the Chinamen's race. At five o'clock people lined each side of the big bridge to enjoy the horse racing. Big Sleepy Jim of Rossland won the free-for-all while the ladies' saddle race "proved as full of excitement as chariot races of old." Miss Graham of Rossland rode long-bodied, long-legged Sleepy Jim who quite outclassed the ponies, Buttons and Vicki.

By now it was almost dusk and Chinese lanterns twinkled amongst evergreen decorations. Band music filled the air and during a pause Mayor Topping spoke from the balcony of the Fire Hall. When the dark deepened, sky rockets and Roman candles provided a display of melting colors and streaking flames in the night sky. For two hours the townspeople revelled in the brilliant show and then made their way to a Grand Ball in the Opera House, a fitting climax to a red-letter day.[10]

In July, 1901, Topping was poised on the crest of his career. As Mayor he presided over the first meetings of the City Council, appointed various committees and organized the method of administration. F. W. Warren was named treasurer while Chief of Police Devitt undertook the offices of city clerk, assessor, collector and health officer. The volunteer fire brigade passed into city control and it was decided to pay the fire chief five dollars and each of his men two dollars and fifty cents for every fire they attended. Many bylaws were enacted, including one which prohibited speed on the bridge greater than a trot or canter. Owners of horses, cattle, dogs and fowl were warned they must keep their stock from running at large. In August the city's seal arrived and official approval could now be given to all bylaws. The seal bore the motto, "Gold Must be Tried by Fire" while the title, "Smelting and Refining", surrounded an engraving of the smelter with ore cars in the foreground. The year ended with city finances in admirable condition. More than one thousand dollars lay in the treasury; all expenses of incorporation had been paid and not a cent was owing.

[10] Trail Creek News, July 6, 1901.

Despite this excellent record, Mayor Topping announced at the last Council meeting in November that he was resigning his office and would not stand for re-election the following year. His health had bothered him and failing eyesight persuaded him to spend the winter at his mining properties in Sheridan Camp. Topping's resignation was to prove a turning point in his career. Leaving the administration of the city to others, he would recede into the background of affairs. A group of younger men would undertake to solve the problems of the community and it would develop under guidance from another quarter.

7.

TRIUMPH FOR TOWN AND SMELTER

T RAIL HAD been born a smelter town and continued existence depended entirely on the survival of its smelter. That was no small problem in the years after the C.P.R. purchase. When W. H. Aldridge arrived to take charge of the Canadian Smelting Works he found competing plants at Pilot Bay, Nelson and Northport, and within two years smelters were built at Grand Forks, Greenwood and Boundary Falls. Ore supplies were not great enough to sustain them all and Canadian laws did not encourage a thriving smelting industry. Aldridge set out to create more favorable conditions by changing the objectionable laws and in his campaign enlisted the help of the Mayor and Council of Trail as well as the local Board of Trade.

He took his first step in this direction during the summer of 1899 when he outlined the problems of the lead industry to the Associated Boards of Trade, meeting in Rossland. Canadian lead bullion was sent to the United States for refining and when readmitted to Canada was subject to duty charges. Some manufactured lead products were protected by a high Canadian tariff but compounds of lead used in the making of paint were admitted free, so no Canadian lead compounds could compete with those from a foreign country. Aldridge considered the ultimate remedy would be to refine and manufacture in Canada all the lead needed in any form but this could not be done unless the tariff were adjusted to provide protection for all kinds of lead produced. Following his suggestions Colonel Topping (as President of the Trail Board of Trade) introduced two resolutions which the Associated Boards adopted and sent to the government in Ottawa. One resolution advocated that lead smelted in Canada and refined in the United States be readmitted into Canada free of duty. The other asked for import duties on lead compounds to match the duties on pipe and shot. The second resolution was rejected but the first won approval and the Dominion government permitted Canadian bullion refined in the States to return free of charge.[1]

Impact in Trail was immediate. The Canadian Smelting Works installed a lead furnace which began operations in January of 1900. Shipments of lead ore began to come in from the Boundary mines, from the Slocan, from Ymir and the North Star in the East Kootenay. The smelter was able to operate more steadily and the monthly payroll rose to sixty thousand dollars in 1901.[2]

American smelting interests did not take kindly to development of a Canadian smelter, so raised the price charged for refining. It became clear that the only solution was to establish a lead refinery in Canada, but without protection this was impossible. Since the government refused any tariff revision, it was decided to ask for a bounty on lead. Accordingly, in March 1901, the Associated Boards passed a resolution (again introduced by Colonel Topping) asking for a bounty of five dollars a ton on lead of Canadian origin smelted and refined in Canada. G. O. Buchanan of Kaslo travelled to Ottawa to present the resolution and in May a graduated series of subsidies was announced. As a result the Canadian Smelting Works decided to build a lead refinery at Trail and Aldridge boldly adopted the new electrolytic process of refining which had

[1] Trail Creek News, Aug. 12, 1899.
[2] Trail Creek News, Oct. 12, Nov. 4, Nov. 25, Dec. 9, Dec. 30, 1899, Jan. 20, Sept. 1, 1900.

been developed recently by Anson G. Betts of Troy, New York. Betts came to Trail to supervise construction. The experiment was successful. Pig lead was shipped in the summer of 1902 and in October of 1903 eighty-five thousand ounces of silver and three hundred ounces of gold were shipped to United States government assay offices — the first shipments ever made from a Canadian refinery.[3]

Still determined to obtain tariff protection on compound lead products, the silver-lead mine owners sent three delegates to Ottawa to press the demand. They were John L. Retallack, L. Pratt and S. S. Fowler. The government refused to change the tariff so the delegates advocated a bounty of fifteen dollars a ton to be paid to the mine owners. This the government granted in July, 1903. To Aldridge the proposal was acceptable for he considered he would get increased smelting business when the bounty was paid to the mine owners. In July 1905 the Dominion government finally reversed its stand, placing a duty on lead compounds to protect Canadian manufactures. Aldridge now decided to make lead pipe and a plant was erected which turned out sixty different sizes and styles up to four inches in diameter.[4]

After a long struggle Aldridge had conquered most of his operating problems by 1905. His policy had been to ensure the reduction and treatment of ores in Canada. He had taken over a small plant worth no more than two hundred thousand dollars in 1898 and raised its value to more than a million dollars. Many improvements had been added. The copper furnaces had been increased from two to four. Open air roasting had given way to covered stalls which improved the dissipation of fumes. Adoption of Huntington-Heberlein roasters for lead ores improved efficiency and reduced the time considerably. Production in the refinery rose from twenty to fifty tons daily. Working hours were reduced from two shifts of eleven and thirteen hours to three eight-hour shifts.

[3] Trail Creek News, Feb. 23, April 20, May 4, May 18, Dec. 28, 1901, July 19, Aug. 16, 1902.
[4] Trail Creek News, Aug. 2, 1902.

For the citizens of Trail the development and expansion meant their livelihood. The editor of the Trail Creek News reflected their attitude when he wrote: "This is what Trail people like to see. The thicker the smoke ascending into the skies from Smelter Hill, the greater is Trail's prosperity." [5]

The years of 1905-06 saw the triumph of Walter H. Aldridge in his effort to establish a smelting industry in Canada and to ensure that the centre of that industry should be in Trail rather than in other smelter towns. Although he had increased the capacity of the Trail plant, cut its costs, expanded it to include a refinery and a lead pipe manufactory, he was plagued by uncertainty in the flow of ores. For economy, operation should be continuous and to attain this Aldridge envisioned a consolidation of the leading mines, their ores to be treated at one smelter. All during 1905 he negotiated with the directors of the LeRoi, the War Eagle, the St. Eugene, the Centre Star to this purpose. The value of the merger was apparent to all and the Trail smelter was favored over the plants at Nelson and Northport because of lower costs. Owners of the War Eagle, Centre Star and St. Eugene finally approved amalgamation but a stormy meeting of LeRoi shareholders voted against the proposition, so the British-American Co. remained outside the deal. The merger was consummated in January, 1906, under the title, Canadian Consolidated Mines Limited, and included the War Eagle, Centre Star and St. Eugene mines, the Rossland Power Company and the Canadian Smelting Works. Incorporated in Toronto, it was capitalized at five million, five hundred thousand dollars. In February, 1906 the name of the new concern was changed to the Consolidated Mining and Smelting Company of Canada Limited.

Officers of the company were W. D. Matthews of Toronto as president, George Sumner of Montreal, vice-president, W. H. Aldridge of Trail, Managing Director. Directors included E. B. Osler and H. S. Osler of Toronto, Charles R. Hosmer of Montreal and W. L. Matthews of Toronto.

[5] Trail Creek News, June 13, 1903, Jan. 7, 1905, Oct. 7, 1905.

In his first report to the management, Aldridge summed up the policy of the new company in these words: "The Consolidated Mining and Smelting Company of Canada Limited is not dependent upon any single mine, nor upon any single mining district; but its interests and business, besides being to an extent industrial, will also be so diversified as to minimize so far as possible, the speculative element."[6] The stage was thus set for development of an enterprise which in later years would attain world-wide significance.

Meanwhile, as the smelter extended its scope, the city council made improvements in the town. Noble Binns succeeded Topping as Mayor in 1902. At the end of the year he was appointed Police Magistrate and resigned as Mayor. He was followed by James Hargrave Schofield who continued as Mayor until 1907 when he was elected to the Provincial Legislative Assembly.[7]

One of the immediate problems concerned Dublin Gulch, a narrow strip of land to the north of the town, lying between two steep hills. Through the Gulch ran Trail Creek and beside it was the railway and the road to Rossland, while settlers had built houses wherever room could be found. In reality they were squatters for the land was part of the railway land grant. Now the squatters were agitating for an arrangement to be made with the C.P.R. whereby they could acquire title to their property. After much negotiation the council reached an agreement with the C.P.R. which deeded to the city thirty feet on each side of their right-of-way in return for land on the hillside.The route of the road was changed; several houses were moved back and by 1903 the city was able to sell lots to the people living there. By the same agreement the Council took possession of the cemetery property on Smelter Hill which had also been railway land.[8]

Heinze had operated a ferry across the Columbia River

[6] Trail Creek News, June 17, March 18, July 1, Aug. 26, Nov. 25, Dec. 9, 1905, Jan. 27, Feb. 24, March 31, 1906.
[7] Trail Creek News, Jan. 18, 1902, Jan. 10, Jan. 17, 1903.
[8] Trail Creek News, March 8, March 15, 1902, Jan. 31, 1903.

while he was building the smelter, but for several years the
craft had lain high and dry on the beach, unused. In the
spring of 1902 the Council decided to put the service in operation again. A ferry company was organized with J. H. Schofield as president and a new barge was built. It was ready
for launching by May and the company cleared ground on the
far side of the Columbia for baseball. George White agreed
to run the ferry and he erected a pole for a flag to be used as a
signal by anyone wishing conveyance from the eastern approach.
Later he replaced the flag with a gong and built a small station
containing a stove and firewood. Although a crossing of the
river was provided by this arrangement, complaints were common. One passenger tartly remarked, "It seems that the Trail
ferry does not run if it is raining, if it is a holiday, if it is
Sunday, or if the ferryman does not feel like it." [9]

Trail had a population of at least two thousand people and
a payroll of seventy-five thousand dollars a month in 1906
but it still possessed many features of a frontier settlement.
Financially sound, it yet presented an appearance not far removed from its earliest days. Boxlike frame stores with false
fronts and verandahs, hotels built on pilings, clustered along
one side of the Columbia River. No settlement had been made
on the far side for the only crossing was by an erratic ferry,
prone to mishap in the swift current. Trail Creek still meandered
over the flats in the heart of the town, providing a wide entrance
for the Columbia in its rampaging floods. During summer the
low-lying bottom lands beneath the two-plank bridges lay use-
less. The sight offended the aldermen, for it made Trail "look
like a city of shacks on stilts stuck in a hole in the ground."
They wished to divert the creek's course and fill the depression
with smelter slag. Those early councils did not accomplish
this but in ten years' time the creek would be contained in a
culvert below ground and the downtown area raised with a
fill of slag so no bridges would be necessary.[10]

[9] Trail Creek News, March 22, April 5, April 12, May 24, June 14,
July 5, Sept. 6, 1902.
[10] Trail Creek News, Nov. 22, 1902.

Stumps were now gone from vacant lots but wooden side-
walks and dusty thoroughfares still remained. Small frame
houses clung precariously to the lower slope of Lookout Mountain while on a bench abve the town stood a neat white
schoolhouse. Spires of a few churches mingled with the big
barnlike halls and down at the river's edge a grandstand and
ballfield were used for sports in summer and a rink in winter.
Only the occasional sternwheeler now called at the boat landing
and the depot which was originally built on the river bank was
moved in 1903 to a spot between Pine and Cedar avenues.
Over all hovered thick yellow smoke from the smelter, its
acrid fumes scorching trees and flowers.

With all the activities in town and smelter, Topping had
little connection. After spending the winter of 1901-2 in
Sheridan Camp he returned to Trail for a brief stay before
going to the Horsefly Camp in the Cariboo. There he prospected
for claims in country so rough he had to carry provisions on
his back. By the autumn he was back in Trail in time to
attend a banquet for veterans returning from the Boer War.
At Christmas time he acted as Santa Claus at the Anglican
church party.

Although still assessed for property valued at more than
five thousand dollars Topping showed his first hint of financial
weakness in the fall of 1902. Twenty-seven lots owned by him
were included in the tax delinquent sale for that year but most
of the taxes were paid before the sale took place.[11]

In September, 1902, the Colonel's nephew, Jim Worth, cut
his foot while working as a timberman in a Rossland mine.
Blood poisoning developed and he lay seriously ill in Mater
Misericordiae Hospital. Gradually the poison spread through
his body and he died early in October. Funeral services were
held in St. Andrew's Church with members of the Rossland
Baseball Club as pallbearers and he was buried beside his wife,
Maud Hanna, in the cemetery on Smelter Flats. A big powerful
man, he had been an excellent ball player and was just twenty-

---

[11] Trail Creek News, Feb. 22, March 15, Sept. 6, Sept. 27, Nov. 1, 1902,
Jan. 3, 1903.

seven years old at the time of his death. Jane Hanna now took complete charge of his two-year-old son.[12]

The closing days of 1903 saw another wedding in the Hanna household. A few days before Christmas, Sophia Hanna was married to Police Chief William John Devitt in St. Andrew's Church. The bride, dressed in a dark travelling costume, was attended by her twin sisters, Molly and Lydia, while Alderman J. P. Byers supported the groom. Mayor Schofield gave the bride away. After the honeymoon, the couple resided in the neat new house built by Devitt at the corner of Cedar and Helena.[13]

To Manager Aldridge, to Mayor Schofield and the aldermen, the year 1906 marked the beginning of a new era but for Colonel Topping it was the end of an adventurous career. He had gradually withdrawn from public life and now financial reverses occupied his attention. Beset by failure in his Lookout Mountain mines, he pinned hopes for reviving his fortune on claims in Sumpter, Oregon. Sumpter Camp had been rich in placer gold in the 1860's and later in the eighties rich lode mines were found. Unfortunately, by the time Topping invested in it the camp was already played out and Topping found no second LeRoi within its bounds. Late in 1904 he was forced to let many of his Trail lots sell for their unpaid taxes. His share of Columbia Heights was taken over by creditors and the remainder of his Lookout claims reverted to the Crown. Very little is recorded of him in these years. The erstwhile Father of Trail was almost forgotten in his town.[14]

However the Colonel made one more appearance before his final exit. Late in the afternoon of a sunny September day in 1906, he and Mary Jane Hanna were united in marriage, not in the city which they had founded and where they had lived for sixteen years, but in neighboring Rossland. On September 21 a small group of old friends gathered in Nelson Burritt's apartment in the Kootenay Hotel where Rev. J. A.

[12] Trail Creek News, Sept. 6, Sept. 27, Oct. 4, Oct. 11, 1902.
[13] Trail Creek News, Jan. 2, 1904.
[14] Trail Creek News, Dec. 12, 1903, Nov. 12, 1904.

Cleland of St. George's Church performed the ceremony. Witnesses were Charles R. Hamilton, Julia G. Burritt, Vaur M. Collins and W. K. Esling. After the wedding "Toppins" and Jane caught the evening train for Revelstoke, the first step on the way to Victoria. Now sixty-two years of age, the Colonel left the Kootenays, never to return. For the next several years his home was in Victoria but mining interests took him occasionally to northern British Columbia where it was reported he was developing claims in the Bulkley River valley.[15]

Death came to Eugene Sayre Topping on January 17, 1917 at the age of seventy-three. Newspaper comment stated that "Few men were better known than Mr. Topping who more than twenty years ago laid out and built the original town of Trail. Although living a retired life in Victoria, he retained much of the buoyant spirit and energy which had characterized his activity in the early years. Colonel Topping was a typical Westerner, big in heart as well as body. He possessed sterling qualities, was well liked and everyone regrets his death."

As for Jane Hanna Topping, little is left to record. Her first husband, Frank Hanna, had long since died in El Paso, Texas. After leaving Trail he had settled on a ranch close to the Mexican border within sound of rebel gunfire during the troubled days of insurrections. Jane lived on to the age of seventy-four years, residing after Colonel Topping's death with her daughter Estella in Ventura, California. Although far from the Kootenays she was remembered as the first white woman to winter in Nelson and to live in the town of Trail. A simple statement in the local press remains to tell us of her: "She was small and dark and much loved for her kindness."

[15] Trail Creek News, Sept. 22, 1906.

8.

EPILOGUE

I N A WAY, Topping, Heinze, and Aldridge in themselves typified the varying phases of Trail's early development. First came Topping when Trail was nothing but a landing-place for miners on their way to Rossland. He was an adventurer, ever pushing on to unknown country, looking for an Eldorado and ever ready to gamble on any chance Fortune offered. That chance came the day he acquired the LeRoi claim and when he shrewdly pre-empted land for a townsite at the mouth of Trail Creek. He became a booster, a salesman, riding the crest of promotional schemes. Lacking the ability required for making a mine, he used his talents to interest the free-wheeling capitalist, F. Augustus Heinze.

Heinze was no prospector. Not for him was the search for claims nor the rough life of the wilds. Rather he saw opportunity in using his money to purchase other men's finds, in consolidating them and turning them into paying propositions. Like Topping he was a gambler, ready for any risk that promised profit. Completely self-interested and determined to succeed, he invested in the Trail Creek area to further his own fortunes, but in so doing built the town and contributed things of permanent value. It took a man like Heinze, supremely confident in his own judgment, to venture on establishing a smelter in the wild isolated country of southern British Columbia. When the first flush of success had passed and difficulties arose, Heinze lost interest and left for greener fields.

The time was then ready for Aldridge, the sound administrator, the man with specialized knowledge and breadth of view who could turn the smelter into a successful business operation. He was not a man of the frontier, seeking fortune as an individual, but a man of the industrial world beyond the mountains where corporate action and management techniques were the way to success. No gambler, as were Topping and Heinze, nevertheless he took risks, but they were calculated risks and turned on knowledge of the basic problems of the industry and on an insight into possibilities for their solution.

After Aldridge's day other men of the same type — executives, scientists, engineers — would carry the smelter to further development by using all the advancing metallurgical and chemical knowledge of their times. Trail would become a mecca for scientists from everywhere — Australia, Africa, Europe, Japan, the United States — wherever minerals were reduced to usable materials or fertilizers made to enrich the earth's soil.

This was a world far beyond that of Eugene Sayre Topping, the "Kentucky colonel", the wanderer, the man of the frontier, but to him must go the credit for initiating it all. He was the founding Father of Trail and its colorful "first citizen".

Eugene Sayre Topping with his grand-nephew, Eugene Frank (Dick) Worth, orphan son of Maud Hanna and Jim Worth, about 1906.

Short, stocky, red-haired Frank Hanna had powerful shoulders and could toss out a drunk in each hand from the barroom of the Trail House.

Dark and vivacious, Mary Jane Hanna resembled her Huguenot mother. Picture taken about 1900.

Hanna children in the summer of 1895. From left—Sophia, Olive, the twins Lydia and Mollie on each side of Frankie Jr., Maud.

A day of celebration in front of the Arlington Hotel about 1899. The Arlington, built in 1896, still serves the travelling public.

McPhee Building at corner of Bay and Helena was built in 1896 and demolished in 1958. It was also known as the Dolan block and the old post-office.

Police Chief W. J. Devitt, assessor, health officer and city clerk, who married Sophia Hanna.

Courtesy of Cominco Magazine

Police Chief Wm. H. Devitt, second from left, in front of jail.

Crown Point Hotel, Trail.

Trail in 1899 showing the Big Bridge over meandering Trail Creek.

F. Augustus Heinze

Aldridge described him as extremely smart, very likeable, a free spender, a real gambler and not above being crooked to serve his ends.

Trail House built by Topping and Hanna in 1894. It burned to the ground in 1908.

First construction work on Heinze's smelter began in the autumn of 1895.

Ore roasting in the open air at the Trail smelter, 1898.

Trail in 1898 with sternwheeler at landing and overhead cable type ferry used for crossing the Columbia River. Smelter with two stacks stands on a bench above the town.

Settler of copper blast furnace with slag flowing into a pot while matte is tapped into a smaller pot, Canadian Smelting Works, 1902 - 1906.

Lead Refinery of Consolidated Mining & Smelting Company of Canada about 1912.

Copper smelter of the British Columbia Smelting & Refining Company, 1896. Built by F. A. Heinze.

General office built by Heinze in 1896 and used by the Canadian Smelting Works. The third rail on the tracks transforms the narrow-gauge to standard width.

First Council of the City of Trail, 1901.

Courtesy of City of Trail

Mayor E. S. Topping

C. A. McAnally

J. P. Byers

J. Dawson

Noble Binns

A. E. Steele

W. Furnell

Horse races on Trail's main street, passing the Hanna Block.

Cleaning an arc light on Bay Avenue about 1900.

Bar of Klondike Hotel on Bay Avenue with John Harkness and owner James W. Harkness and unidentified patron in 1905.

Smelter team in firemen's hose reel race on Dominion Day, 1902. Leading man is Anson Betts, inventor of the electrolytic process for refining lead which was first used by the Canadian Smelting Works at Trail.

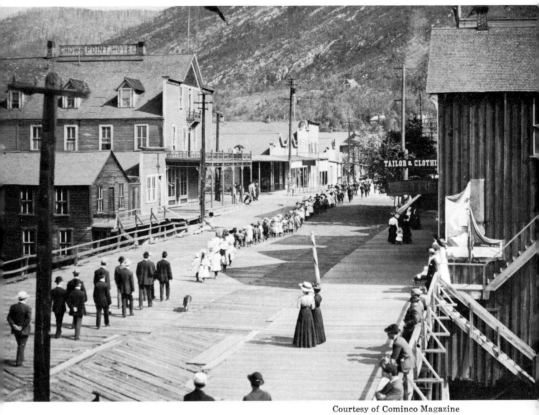

The big Bay Avenue Bridge provided ample space for a parade in 1906.

A picnic party about 1908.

Walter Hull Aldridge, manager of the Canadian Smelting Works, dressed for tennis in 1910.

W. H. Aldridge surrounded by the staff of the Canadian Smelting Works in his residence in 1905. Back row—Chas. Biesel, James McDougall, Clarence McDougall, F. W. Guernsey, W. E. Purcell, S. G. Blacklock (rear), George Morin. Middle row—J. Buchanan, John Miller, W. H. Aldridge, J. M. Turnbull, R. H. Stewart. Front row—H. E. Dodge, A. J. McNab, G. F. Weir, T. W. Bingay.

The Georgetti family and friends enjoy a party Italian Style with wine and coffee.

Coffee and wine for the ladies in the parlor of the Crown Point Hotel. From left—Mrs. Dominic Priore, Mrs. Mike Georgetti, Mrs. Daniel Martinelli.

The steamer "Lytton", crowded with picnickers, as she nosed on to a beach on the Arrow Lake.

Locomotive which ran on the narrow-gauge line of the Columbia & Western between Trail and Rossland from 1896 to 1899.

Decorated with flags and bunting the first train over the newly constructed Columbia & Western line from Robson pulls into Smelter Junction in October, 1897 with Robert B. Graham in the cab of the locomotive.

A typical sunny day at Trail, B.C., along the banks of the Columbia River, with Cominco's metallurgical plants in the background. White "smoke" seen arising from the stacks is vaporized ammonium sulphate used to scrub or clean sulphur dioxide bearing gases. Ammonium sulphate is a fertilizer.